BIBLICAL CHRISTIANITY

BIBLICAL
CHRISTIANITY

An easier-to-read and abridged version of the classic
"Institutes of the Christian Religion" by John Calvin
first published in 1536.

Prepared by B.R. Wood, B.A., B.D.,
(from the English summary by J.P. Wiles, M.A., entitled:
"Instruction in Christianity", published in 1920)

General Editor — J.K. Davies, B.D.

© GRACE PUBLICATIONS TRUST
139 Grosvenor Avenue
LONDON N5 2NH

First Published
1982

4th Impression 1997

ISBN 0 9505476 7 0

Distributed by: EVANGELICAL PRESS
12 Wooler Street Darlington
Co. Durham DL1 1RQ

*Cover design–the alpine Gentian, by
John Shakespeare. This flower was chosen
because of Calvin's association
with Geneva.*

Printed and bound in Great Britain
by Cox & Wyman Ltd, Reading, Berkshire.

CONTENTS

Ascension.
Coronation.
Return.
Judgment.

(N.B. Calvin wrote a part iv, on the Church, its sacraments, and its government, which has not been included in this book).

PART I:

THE KNOWLEDGE OF GOD THE CREATOR.

Section 1. The knowledge of God and the knowledge of ourselves are closely connected.

If we wish to have real wisdom we must know two things: we must know God and we must know ourselves. In order to know one of these properly we must also know the other.

Knowing God. We cannot think seriously about ourselves without thinking about the One who made us, and continues to care for us. The powers we have are such that we could not have made them ourselves, and we most certainly could not have given ourselves life. We have been given so many things in this life, that we must think of the Giver. More than this, the evil of our natures makes us turn to God seeking for better things. We want him to replace our ignorance, poverty, weakness and corruption with his true wisdom, wealth, power and righteousness.

Knowing ourselves. In order to have a right knowledge of ourselves, we must know God and know what we are like in God's sight. Our human pride makes us think we are wise and holy, until we look to the Lord, whose perfection is the only standard we must be measured against. Then we find that we are hypocrites. We are content to *appear* to be righteous without having God's true righteousness. Our judgment is tainted by evil around us. Because of this, we think certain things are good when, in fact, it's only that they are not so corrupt as other things. In the same way, we may look from black to cream colour and, because our eyes are adjusted to the black, we think the cream is white. We need to learn that in God's sight our righteousness is sin, our strength is weakness, and our wisdom is folly.

The reactions of those who met God. Saints who were conscious of the presence of God were filled with fear and amazement. Samson's father, Manoah, said: "We shall surely die, for we have seen God" (Judges 13:22). Isaiah felt very strongly his own uncleanness. He cried out: "Woe is me! For I am lost; for I am a man of unclean lips" (Isaiah 6:5). See also Ezeh 1:28; 3:14; Daniel 8:18; 10:16,17. From these people we can learn that man has a sense of his own worthlessness when he is faced with the majesty of God.

Section 2. The meaning of knowing God.

To know God is not just to know that there is a God. God is not truly known by people who do not live a godly life. Some people know a little of God when they know that he created all things by his power and maintains them as they are. Some even realise that he governs mankind with wisdom, justice and loving care. But we can only truly know God when we also know that we have no wisdom, righteousness, power or truth except from him. We need to seek all good things from him and thank him. Then we will realise that, since he made and keeps us, our lives belong to him. If we are his, our actions should be only what he wants us to do. We would turn away from sin. Our desiring to do good would not be from fear of punishment if we did wrong, but because we love him and fear to offend him.

Section 3. The knowledge of God is naturally planted in man's mind.

It is a fact of life that cannot be questioned that there is some thought of a god of some kind in every human mind. God has given and continues to give this conviction. Men have no excuse that they did not know there is a God. Even the fact that people bow down to idols proves they think there is a God, someone above them who is worthy of worship.

We can easily see, then, that religion was not invented, as some critics have said, to keep down the common people. It is true that some have used religion to do this, but they could never have done so unless men had thoughts of God already deep in their minds. Some people may claim they believe there is no God, yet even they find times when they are forced to believe in a God they wish to forget. They fear punishment for their evil deeds.

The knowledge of God is not something a man learns at school. He finds this knowledge within himself, and he cannot completely remove this truth from himself, no matter how hard he may try.

Section 4. This knowledge is stifled or corrupted by ignorance and wickedness.

While it is an indisputable fact that men have some idea that there is a God, very few treasure this thought. Some people are superstitious. Others deliberately choose wickedness. They are not just foolish. They have rebelled against God. Even if they think about God, they do not have a high enough opinion of him. With all this wrong view of God, they think they are being wise. Paul says: "Professing themselves to be wise, they became fools" (Romans 1:22).

13

David describes those who stifle the light God has given them when he says: "The fool has said in his heart, There is no God" (Psalm 14:1). Some of the wicked say there is no God. Others *act* as if there is no God. These David describes when he says (Psalm 36:2,10,11) that there is no fear of God before the eyes of the wicked, and that they flatter themselves in their evil ways with the imagination that God does not see them. At the same time, even those who wish to banish God from their hearts are faced at times by God's standard of judgment. This judgment within them is the conscience.

Some think it doesn't matter what we believe so long as we try hard. But God doesn't change. His standards of right and wrong are not altered just to suit us. God must be known in the only right way or otherwise our view of him will be so wrong it would be better not to have it at all. The apostle Paul tells the Ephesians that they were without God, so long as they erred from the right knowledge of the only true God. This is true of us. If we do not know God in the right way, we might as well worship idols.

Never to think of God unless we are forced to is also sinful. The fear sinners have for him is forced from them by their fear of his judgment. They would even like to reverse his just decisions. Yet some of these same people make an outward show of being religious, while at the same time they are committing all kinds of sin.

There ought to be regular obedience to him through the whole of life, but sinners rebel against him by doing wicked things. Then they think they can regain his favour by a few sacrifices. By such evil-doing the sparks of the knowledge of God are extinguished. Such people lose what knowledge God gave them about himself. In good times they mock God. In bad times they turn to him in despair. Their prayers at such times show they are not entirely ignorant of him.

Section 5. God can be known through the working of the universe.

God shows himself in the structure of the universe so clearly that men need only open their eyes to see him in his works. It is true that men cannot fully grasp his essence, for it is hidden from them. But there are clear and certain marks of his glory in what he has made. We have no excuse for not knowing him. We may turn our eyes to whatever part of creation we wish and see it glisten with something of the glory he has given it. The apostle Paul tells us (Romans 1:19) that God has shown himself to men in the works of his hands, so that the invisible things of him — his eternal power and Godhead — are clearly seen, being understood by the things that are made.

There are so many things that show his wisdom. It is true that scientists can now search more deeply into the secrets of divine wisdom. They can use their knowledge to observe the movement of the stars and planets, sun and moon. They can measure their distance and admire their grandeur. But that does not mean that we who are not scientists have an excuse for not recognising the maker of these things. We have eyes. We can see how many, how varied and how orderly these heavenly bodies are. Quite clearly, God has revealed his wisdom in his wonderful works to ALL mankind.

In the same way, it takes a carefully trained doctor fully to recognise the structure, beauty and usefulness of the human body. Yet it is admitted by all that the framework of the body proves the great skill of its maker. Truly "God is not far from every one of us" (Acts 17:27). Now, if we only need go as far as our own body to find the handiwork of God, we are inexcusable in our laziness if we refuse to seek him. In fact this shows just how ungrateful men are. They have within themselves God's great works and immeasurable gifts, and swell with pride that they are so gifted. They should be praising the giver.

Men have used the word "nature" so that they do not have to think about God. They say that "nature" was the maker of all these wonderful things, everything from their eyes to the tips of their finger-nails. Most of all the swift working of a man's mind, his splendid powers of reasoning show plainly his creator. And yet men use these God-given powers to war against him.

Some people say the soul cannot exist without the body. Thus it would die when the body dies. But the soul does function independently of the body. It is nothing to do with the body when we study the skies. It is not with our bodies that we can consider past and future, remember what we have heard, hold a picture in our minds, and even have in our minds thoughts and pictures when we are asleep. These are further signs of God's handiwork in man. The marks of immortality can never be wiped from human nature. Surely man's own reason must compel him to acknowledge a creator.

Other men have tried to remove the idea of a true God by saying there is some sort of universal mind that gives life to the universe. This just replaces God with a shadowy power, and to such a power it would not be proper to give fear and worship. In matters of such importance, it is a mistake of serious consequences to confuse God with the things he has made, and with the workings of nature which are subject to his will.

We should therefore remember, whenever we think of our bodies, that there is one God who governs all things. It is his desire that we turn to him, believe on him and worship him. It is against all sound reason to use and enjoy the great gifts he has given us and turn away from the giver who continues to give us all we need.

Let us admire God's wonderful works. By his power he

holds up the heaven and earth. He makes the sky shake with thunder, and lights it up with lightning. He stirs up the air with storms and calms them in a moment. He gives a boundary to the roaring waves of the sea, lashes them up to fury with wild winds and again brings peace. The power of God leads us to think of his eternity. He from whom all things come, must be eternal. He must have existence within himself.

We can also see God's work in human affairs. He is kind to all men, and yet he shows his working in such a way that he is plainly and constantly good to the righteous and severe to the wicked. He shows himself in punishment of crime, and just as clearly as protector and avenger of innocence. The fact that he sometimes allows the wicked to triumph for a while and allows the innocent to suffer hardship and be oppressed by the wicked, does not hide his justice. In contrast to this thought, we should learn when he punishes one crime, that he hates all crimes. And when we see that he leaves many for the present unpunished, we should learn that there is a judgment to come, when they will be punished.

The psalmist teaches us about God's care in Psalm 107. There he tells us how God gave marvellous and unexpected help to the unhappy, protected and guided those wandering in the desert, gave food to the hungry, delivered prisoners from captivity, healed the sick, gave fertility to the earth, and raised the people who had been brought low. Many people think such events are the result of chance, but the Psalmist shows they are God's care for his own people. He adds that those who realise this will understand the loving-kindness of the Lord.

When we truly know God, we will look forward to the future life. When we know that God's present goodness and severity are incomplete, we must conclude that this life is only the beginning. There will be a fuller display of mercy and judgment in the world to come. When we see godly people suffer affliction from the wicked, while the wicked live in comfort, we are right to think there will be another life when both good and bad will receive the treatment that is right for them.

Augustine wisely said: "If every sin were now visited with punishment we might think that there was no judgment to come; and if no sin were immediately punished we might think that there was no such thing as divine power and care".

In spite of the fact that God clearly displays his immortal power in his handiwork, mankind does not learn from the lesson. We do not look often on the natural things around and think of the maker. We, too often, speak of events as chance, instead of realising they are God's work. The works of creation shine around us like lamps to show forth the glory of their maker. But they shine in vain. We do not take enough notice of them. But because they are there, we cannot say we had no way to know God. However, God has most graciously given us another guide, a brighter light, to bring us to the true knowledge of our creator. That light is the scriptures.

Section 6.   Man needs the scriptures to reach a true knowledge of his creator.

Although God shows us the splendour of his glory in creation so that we have no excuse for not knowing him, we need better help to know God in the right way. Therefore, he has given us the light of his Word. That is a privilege for those to whom he wishes to make himself more intimately known.

A person who has poor sight may be quite unable to read two words in a book, but if he uses spectacles he will be able

18

to read easily. It is like this with the scriptures. They clear our blurred knowledge of God and reveal him distinctly. Because of this, the Bible is a most precious gift. God has given us written information so that we are not left to search for him in the works of creation alone.

God made himself known to the writers of scripture by spoken words, by visions and by teaching them what to write. But with all these means, they were sure of the truth of the teaching they received, and certain that it came from God. God placed his truth above suspicion. These truths were made into a written public record for later generations to use. The main aim of the books of the law and the prophets was to testify of Christ; but scripture also served to distinguish the true God, the creator of heaven and earth, from the whole multitude of false gods.

We can say definitely, then, that it is right for man to consider God's glory as he shows it in creation. It is also right to read the Word of God. In fact, we must read it if we wish to increase our knowledge of our creator. We cannot learn anything at all of sound doctrine unless we learn from the holy scriptures.

When we remember how quickly the human mind forgets God, we can see how great was the need for his truth to be written down. If we do not know his Word, we shall never reach our goal of knowing God. It is of interest to note that the same prophet who tells us that the heavens declare the glory of God and that the constant succession of days and nights proclaims his majesty, afterwards goes on to say: "The law of the Lord is perfect, converting the soul; the testimony of the Lord is sure, making wise the simple" (Psalm 19).

Section 7.   The Holy Spirit guarantees the authority of scripture.

Believers need to know for certain that the scriptures have come from heaven. It is a serious error to say that scripture owes all its importance to the sanction of the church. The eternal and unchangeable truth of God does not depend on the judgment of man. The Church has said it should decide what should be included in the Bible.* But this is merely because the Church wishes simple people to think it is all-powerful. We do not depend on the judgment of men. If we did, a man with a troubled conscience would have only other men to turn to. But he can turn to the scriptures to find hope of eternal life.

Paul tells us that the church is built on the foundation of the apostles and prophets. If we accept this as true, we must realise that what they wrote in the scriptures was accepted as true doctrine before the building up of the Church. Yes, the scriptures had authority before the Church.

In scripture the highest argument is: "Thus says the Lord". The prophets and apostles do not boast of their own wisdom. They put forward the sacred name of God that it may compel obedience. If we wish to deliver men's consciences from doubt and uncertainty, we must have as the ground of our faith something higher than arguments and decisions of men. This higher ground of faith is the witness of the Holy Spirit within us.

It is of no use to try to encourage belief in the scriptures merely by argument. Even if you do persuade your hearer to accept the scriptures, he is only doing it mentally. Argument will not establish the steadfast faith necessary for godliness.

Men of the world think that religion is in the mind. They

---

*Calvin is talking about the Roman Catholic church of his day.

20

ask to be convinced by strong arguments that Moses and the prophets spoke by divine inspiration. I reply that the witness of the Spirit is above all arguments. The only way we can know God is through what he has said of himself in the scriptures. In the same way, his scriptures will be accepted in the hearts of men only when they are witnessed to by the Holy Spirit. The same Spirit who spoke through the prophets must enter our hearts to convince us that they wrote faithfully the message given them. Isaiah states this clearly: "My spirit that is upon thee, and my words which I have put in thy mouth, shall not depart out of thy mouth, nor out of the mouth of thy seed, nor out of the mouth of thy seed's seed, saith the Lord, from henceforth and for ever" (Isaiah 59:21).

This should be clearly accepted. The man who is inwardly taught by the Spirit relies firmly on the scriptures. Scripture is its own proof. It needs no proof or argument by man. The truth of scripture is testified to us by the Holy Spirit. There could be no greater witness.

By its own majesty scripture commands our reverence, but this makes no real difference to us until we are taught by the Spirit. Then we are enlightened by his power. It is neither by our own judgment nor by that of other men that we believe the scripture to be from God. The Holy Spirit makes us certain that God himself speaks to us in scripture having used chosen men as writers.

Section 8.   There are solid rational proofs to confirm the truth of holy scripture.

Only after we have this certainty through the Holy Spirit, and have embraced scripture with a reverence suited to its dignity, do rational arguments become aids to faith. Our faith is confirmed wonderfully when we consider the order and arrangement of the abundance of divine wisdom in the Bible. We see the unearthly purity of its doctrine and the beauty of all its part. Our hearts are still more confirmed when we observe that our admiration is excited not by beauties of language but by the dignity of the things revealed.

God's wisdom is shown in that the great mysteries of the kingdom of heaven are told usually in a simple style. No man can claim that the power of the words lies in beauty of language. The truths are too mighty to need the artificial help of skilful words. Paul uses this fact when he stated to the Corinthians that their faith stood not in the wisdom of man but in the power of God, because his preaching had not been with enticing words of man's wisdom, but in demonstration of the Spirit and of power (I Corinthians 2:4).

There is a power in scripture that is found in no human writings, however great the beauty of their language. Other books may attract or delight you, but the Word of God can enter into your heart and take hold of your inmost feelings.

Some of the prophets did write with an elegant polished style, with a beauty that can stand beside that of the world's great writers. In this way the Holy Spirit shows that it would have been just as possible to use it always. But the majesty of God is seen as clearly in the ordinary language of Jeremiah and Amos as in the beautiful language of David and Isaiah.

Some proofs of the authority of the Old Testament. Moses is shown to be truthful when we find that he includes information that is not complimentary to his own family. He was a member of the family of Levi, yet he wrote: "Simeon and Levi are brethren; instruments of cruelty are in their habitations" (Genesis 49:5). And he could have avoided telling of the grumblings of his own brother and sister, but he faithfully records it (Numbers 12:1).

He writes about many, many miracles. People who question whether these really happened should notice the fact that nobody disagreed when Moses proclaimed these before the congregation. He could not have given a false account when these people were eye-witnesses of the events. But no people objected when he recorded the manna from heaven, the water from the rock, the cloud over the tabernacle or the thunder when God spoke from the mountain.

At the time Isaiah wrote, Judah was at peace, but he proclaimed the destruction of Jerusalem and exile and even the deliverer Cyrus. This was written an hundred years before the birth of Cyrus. Jeremiah foretold that the captivity would be for seventy years, at a time before they were even taken captive.

Some proofs of the authority of the New Testament. Three of the gospel writers tell the story in a simple, unadorned style, and yet even within these the sermons of Christ are worthy of all our admiration. The writings of Paul and Peter compel our admiration. We see men made new when we remember that Matthew came from the tax office, Peter and John from their fishing boats, while Paul was an open enemy and cruel persecutor of Christians.

God has preserved his written Word for us through thousands of years. He has kept it as his written witness to himself.

Section 9.   It is contrary to God's will for men to neglect scripture and seek fresh revelations.

There are some people who proudly claim to be led by the Holy Spirit. These despise the people who cling to the "dead and killing letter". If they claim to be led by the Spirit of God, it is foolish to think this revelation would be any different from that given to the apostles and prophets who wrote the Word of God.

Paul had once been caught up to the third heaven. He had a right, if anyone had, to claim that he had a special revelation, but he still used scripture and encouraged Timothy to do so. He honours scripture in saying it is "profitable for doctrine, for reproof, for correction, for instruction in righteousness: that the man of God may be perfect, throughly furnished unto all good works" (II Timothy 3:16,17).

When our Lord promised his Holy Spirit, he said he would be one who would not speak of himself, but call to remembrance what Christ himself had taught by spoken words. So the promised Spirit will not give new, unheard-of revelations. He will confirm in our hearts the very same doctrine which the gospel of Christ has given us.

Let this be clear. Those who wish to receive profit and blessing from the Spirit of God must be diligent in reading scripture and in listening to its voice.

To people who say it is an indignity for the Spirit of God who is above all things to be subject to scripture, you may reply that it is no dishonour to the Spirit to be consistent with himself. He is the author of scripture and he cannot change.

To say that those who adhere to the scripture are in bondage to the "killing letter" is playing with words. When Paul said that the letter kills (II Corinthians 3:6) he was opposing false apostles who still clung to the law and would not accept God's new law of grace through Christ. The law does kill when it is separated from the grace of Christ. When it is powerfully impressed on the heart by the Spirit and sets forth Christ, it is the Word of Life.

Real reverence for the Word takes possession of our

hearts when the light of the Spirit enables us to see God in the scriptures; and on the other hand, we welcome without fear of delusion that Spirit which we recognise by his likeness to his own Word.

Section 10.   Creation and scripture agree against the gods of the nations.

We have stated that creation bears witness to God, and that he is more fully revealed in scripture. We must show now that the God of creation is the same as the God of scripture.

In the Bible we see him constantly with the goodness of a father. He delights in showing loving-kindness to his own, but he also shows severity against offenders. Moses appears to have given us a brief account of all we need to know of God: "The Lord, the Lord God, merciful and gracious, longsuffering, and abundant in goodness and truth, keeping mercy for thousands, forgiving iniquity and transgression and sin, and that will by no means clear the guilty; visiting the iniquity of the fathers upon the children, and upon the children's children, unto the third and to the fourth generation" (Exodus 34:6,7). The name "Lord" (Jehovah) spoken twice, shows his eternity and self-existence. Then Moses tells us God's attributes, pointing out what he is in relation to us.

The same attributes are seen to shine in creation: gentleness, goodness, mercy, justice, judgment, truth. Yes, all the attributes of God may be clearly traced in the works of creation.

Then we should notice that scripture expressly rejects all the gods of the nations. We are led to the only true God. The name of God has been everywhere well known. Even those who worshipped many gods still used the name god.

25

But all men have fallen into error and sin, and their natural knowledge of God only serves to make them without excuse. Thus the prophet Habakkuk condemns all idol-worship and tells us to seek God in his holy temple (Habakkuk 2:20). In this way we would not accept any other god than the true God, who has revealed himself in his own Word.

Section 11. It is wrong to make any kind of picture or image of God.

Whenever a man makes any kind of shape and says that this is like God, he is spoiling God's glory with a lie. God has said: "Thou shalt not make unto thee any graven image, or any likeness of any thing that is in heaven above, or that is in the earth beneath, or that is in the water under the earth" (Exodus 20:4). He forbide all attempts to represent him in visible shape.

Moses said: "Therefore take good heed to yourselves. Since you saw no form on the day that the Lord spoke to you at Horeb out of the midst of the fire, beware lest you act corruptly by making a graven image for yourselves in the form of any figure" (Deuteronomy 4:15,16). Moses points out that only God's *voice* was heard. There was no visible shape. All who try to give God a shape are insulting him.

Paul gives the same command when he says: "Being then God's offspring, we ought not to think that the Godhead is like unto gold or silver, or stone, graven by art and man's device" (Acts 17:29). It is obvious that any statue or picture made to represent God is an extreme insult to his great majesty.

There were certain occasions when God did show himself by signs, but these were of a very special kind. In fact they reminded those who saw them that he was beyond their understanding. When the law was given, people saw cloud and smoke and flame. These were signs of his glory, but most certainly signs that were not to be copied by man. In the gospels, the Holy Spirit appeared as a dove, but then he disappeared. This reminds us that God is invisible.

Man, who is himself a created being, cannot give godhead to clay, stone, wood, or even gold or silver. Isaiah shows how foolish it is to choose one piece of metal or wood and call it a god and not the piece next to it (Isaiah 44:12-17). "He plants a cedar and the rain nourishes it. Then it becomes fuel for a man; he takes a part of it and warms himself, he kindles a fire and bakes bread; also he makes a god and worships it, he makes it a graven image and falls down before it" (Isaiah 44:14,15).

Note, also, that God has forbidden picture-idols just as much as carved images. He has forbidden men to make any likeness of himself.

Some people say that images are like books for the common people. People who cannot read need to be reminded of God. It is true that people need to be told of God, but he has expressly forbidden images. They are even forbidden for teaching. Habakkuk said: "The molten image is a teacher of lies". God has his own way of teaching. People who cannot read should be taught by the preaching of his Word. People should be thoroughly taught. There is no need for images of wood, clay, silver and gold. Without these things people can know that Christ died in order that he might bear the curse for us, take our punishment on the cross and atone for our sins by sacrificing his own body to wash away our sins with his blood and reconcile us to God his Father.

It is quite wrong to think that one may worship God in the image and not the image itself. This argument is even used by the heathen. They say of their idolatry that they do not worship the image but what it represents. The same argument is used by the Roman Catholics. They claim that they do "service" to images but do not worship them. This would mean they were servants of idols. This is clearly NOT what God planned when he made mankind.

Section 12.   Worship must be given to God alone.

Whenever lies and wrong beliefs have prevailed, religion has been spoiled and perverted. A disgraceful ignorance is shown when men will not hold fast their belief in the one true God and worship him in the only right way. Yet God has purposely said that he is a jealous God. He will punish those who give to idols the glory that is due to him alone. One of his reasons for giving the ten commandments was that he wanted to prevent men from turning to corrupt worship. If we do not honour God with all the worship that he deserves, we are robbing him of his glory and insulting him.

Superstition offers many tricks to side-track us from pure worship. We must take notice of them. We are tempted to follow strange gods, but without appearing to forsake the one true God. Superstition grants to the one God the highest place, but then adds many smaller gods and gives them certain rights and powers. This breaks up and spreads about the glory of the Godhead. This glory is rightly due to one being only — God. In the same way, the Roman Catholics take from the glory of God by giving honour to angels and saints. These are worshipped, praised and prayed to, and people do not even realise that God's glory is being given to another.

Christ stated this matter very definitely when he said: "Thou shalt worship the Lord thy God, and him only shalt thou serve". This was his rule of action. We can see this when he was tempted to worship another (Matthew 4:10).

We can consider the action of Cornelius (Acts 10:25). He fell at the feet of Peter and worshipped him. Surely he knew enough to know that worship belongs to God alone. If he was looking on Peter as a sign of God's presence and not really worshipping him, this would be worship of the kind that many people think they offer to lesser gods and saints. But Peter strongly forbids Cornelius from kneeling to him. The reason for this must be that man cannot sufficiently distinguish between the worship of God and the worship of a creature without giving the creature some of the honour which belongs to God alone. Let us not rob God of the smallest particle of his glory.

Section 13.   God is one in essence, and this essence contains three Persons.

The nature of God.   The scripture teaches that God is one infinite being, and that he is a spirit being. God speaks only a little about his own essence, but these two characteristics stop us from trying to define him. His infiniteness makes us realise we cannot measure him. The fact that he is a spirit being makes us realise that we cannot describe him in earthly words at all. He is far above all our earthly thoughts.

Some people think of God as if he were human, because the scripture speaks of him as having mouth, ears, eyes, hands and feet. These ways of speaking are only because our human minds cannot think of someone who does not have a visible form. He uses such words in the Bible to help us think of him; and certainly God can see, hear and act. But he does not have a body.

Three distinct persons in one God.   We must understand

29

clearly and must always hold on to this fact that God is one being, but that in the one God three Persons can be known and distinguished. The essence of God is simple and can't be divided. In Hebrews 1:3, Christ is described as the express image of the Father's person. This is not speaking of the essence of God. There is only the one essence. But it does give to Christ a subsistence in which he differs from the Father. We are told that the Son is the brightness of the Father's glory. The character of the Father shines forth in the Son. We conclude therefore that the Son has a separate personality in order to shine forth. The same is true of the Holy Spirit. He can be distinguished from the Father as a separate personality. So we believe the apostle's teaching that there are three Persons in the Godhead.

Errors to avoid. Some teachers have held that Christ was God and the Son of God, but stated that Christ was created. This could not possibly be when Christ is one in essence with the Father. Christ could not have had a beginning. This is why we state so definitely that the Godhead is one essence.

Some people have said that when we speak of the Father, Son and Holy Spirit this just means different attributes of deity. These attributes would be similar to other attributes of God such as wisdom, might and justice. In this view the Father, Son and Spirit are not distinguished. Defenders of the truth have countered this with the clear statement that there are, in the unity of the Godhead, three Persons.

Here is another wrong teaching. It is that Christ began to be when God spoke at the creation. The apostle James tells us that in God there is no change. We must never think that Christ had a beginning at creation. He was begotten of God before time began and was eternally with him. Christ has in himself eternity, self-existence and Godhead.

30

The meaning of person. The word 'person' as used here means one who has a 'subsistence' in the 'essence' (the being) of God and is distinguished from the other members of the Godhead by features of his character and work that are distinctly his own. This word 'subsistence' is meant to indicate something different from what is purely 'essence' or 'being' of God. If Christ was simply God and had nothing distinctly himself, John could not have been correct when he said: "the Word was with God". But he reminds us immediately of the unity of the divine essence by saying: "and the Word was God".

When we speak of God, then, we speak as truly of the Son and the Spirit as we do of the Father. When the Father and Son are mentioned distinctly ("the Father loves the Son", or "the Father sent the Son"), each divine person is distinguished from the others. The work of the Son cannot be attributed to the Father or the Spirit. We cannot say that the Father became man and suffered, or that the Spirit said: "This is my beloved Son".

Proofs from scripture of the Godhead of the Son. When the Bible speaks of 'the Word of God' the phrase does not mean just a voice or even a prophecy. The Word of God is the eternal wisdom that is with God. Now I Peter 1:11 says, about the prophets who wrote the Old Testament, that they were "inquiring what person or time was indicated by the Spirit of Christ within them when predicting the sufferings of Christ and the subsequent glory". At the time of those prophecies, Christ had not appeared in the world. So that statement must refer to Christ as the eternal Word, who had always been with the Father. When we know that the Spirit that spoke by the prophets was the Spirit of Christ, we know with certainty that Christ is God.

The apostles teach that the worlds were made by the Son and he upholds all things by the word of his power

(Hebrews 1:2). Christ himself says: "My Father is working still, and I am working" (John 5:17). In the beginning of John's gospel this teaching is even clearer. The Word, which from the beginning was God and with God, is together with the Father the cause of all things. It is clear here that the Word is eternal, a distinct person, and the agent of all creation. All the revelations from God may be called his Word, but the highest dignity must be given to the *Word*, God's greatest revelation of himself, for the Word is God.

There are proofs of the deity of Christ in the Old Testament. Psalm 45 is speaking of Christ the Messiah when it says: "Thy throne, O God, is for ever and ever". Isaiah 9:6 speaks of Christ as the "Mighty God, the everlasting Father, the Prince of Peace"; and Isaiah also calls him "Emmanuel, God with us". When Jeremiah prophesies the promised Son of David, he says: "This is the name whereby he shall be called, Jehovah, our righteousness". Yes, it is plain the great names for God belong as rightly to the Son as to the Father.

There are many, many witnesses to the Godhead of Christ in the New Testament. Here are some of them: The New Testament views the Old Testament prophecies of acts of God as fulfilled in Christ. Paul asserts that Isaiah's prophecy that the Lord would be a stone of stumbling to Judah (Isaiah 8:14) is fulfilled in Christ (Romans 9:33). Paul also states this: "We must all stand before the judgment seat of Christ. For it is written, As I live, saith the Lord, every knee shall bow to me, and every tongue confess to God". So here again we see that Christ is the fulfilment of prophecy. This is even clearer when the writer to the Hebrews speaks of Christ with a glory with belongs only to God: "Thou, Lord, in the beginning hast laid the foundation of the earth, and the heavens are the works of thine hands". Yes, certainly, the New Testament gives witness that Christ was God. Thomas was right when he cried: "My Lord and my God".

The works of Christ are a further proof that he is God. Even the Pharisees, who rejected his sayings so often, recognised that he claimed to be God when he said: "My Father is working still, and I am working". They wanted to kill him because "he said that God was his Father, making himself equal with God".

His miracles are done in his own name. None but God could do this. In fact, he could, on his own authority, give to others the power to work miracles, to cure lepers and cast our devils (Matthew 10:8; Mark 3:15). Peter said: "In the name of Jesus Christ, arise and walk" (Acts 3:6).

Proofs from scripture of the Godhead of the Holy Spirit. Moses makes this fact clear at the beginning of Genesis when he says that in creation the Spirit moved upon the face of the deep. The Spirit, even at the beginning, used his energy for good when the world was in chaos. In Isaiah 48:16 there is a proof that cannot be questioned. God the Father and the Holy Spirit are spoken of as together doing a work, not just the Father working through the Spirit. "And now the Lord God has sent me and his Spirit". The Spirit shares the supreme authority. His energy is not borrowed. He is the author of both regeneration and immortality. We know that God does not take counsel with any created being, yet the Spirit "searches the deep things of God". The Spirit justifies us by faith. From him come might, truth, sanctification, grace, and every blessing possible. Paul states clearly that the Spirit has both authority and will. He could only have these because he is a person of the Godhead and wholly divine. This is what Paul says: "All these are inspired by one and the same Spirit, who apportions to each one individually as he wills" (I Corinthians 12:11).

When the scripture speaks of the Spirit, it does not hesitate to call him God. Paul knows that the *Spirit* dwells in us, so he says that we are the temple of *God.* In fact, God promised many times to choose us for his temple, and the fulfilment of the promise is completely in this truth, that his Spirit dwells in us. When Peter reproves Ananias for having lied to the Holy Ghost, he adds: "You have not lied to men but to God" (Acts 5:3,4).

The unity of God. There is one God. Paul says in Ephesians 4:5,6: there is "one Lord, one faith, one baptism, one God and Father of us all, who is above all and through all and in all". We are baptized by faith into one true God, and yet at the same time Christ has commanded that we be baptised in the name of the Father, the Son and the Holy Spirit. This one God has revealed himself with perfect clearness as Father, Son and Holy Spirit.

The distinction in the Trinity. This is a great mystery. We must be careful always to speak reverently of this great truth. A Christian scholar of long ago, Gregory of Nazianzum, said: "No sooner do I consider the One, then I am surrounded by the glory of the Three; no sooner do my thoughts distinguish the Three, than they are carried back to the One". We should never think of the Godhead in any way that makes us see God as only *one*, nor as only the *three.*

The words Father, Son and Holy Spirit are not just names. They stand for a real distinction. But it is a distinction without division. It would not be possible to say that the Son was "with God" or that he had a "glory with the Father", if he was the same person as the Father. The Father did not come into the world, but the Son did. It was the Son who died and rose again. And the distinction between Father and Son did not begin when the Son became man. The only begotten Son was in the bosom of the Father in all eternity and has his own glory with the Father. There is also clearly a distinction between the Father and the Spirit, for the Bible says he proceeds from the Father. And the Spirit is not the same as Christ. Christ calls him "another": "Behold, I send you another Comforter".

There is a distinction of work between the persons of the Godhead. The Father is the beginning of working, the fount of all things. The Son has the wisdom and counsel and the dispensation of all government. The Spirit has the power which is active in the world. But we must not over-emphasise this distinction of working.

The eternity of the Father is also the eternity of the Son and of the Spirit and there is no priority of one over the other; yet we do use an order in speaking of the divine persons. And it is right that we do so. The Father is to be reckoned first. The Son is from him. The Spirit is from them both. We can know that the Spirit is from both the Father and the Son from Romans 8. Here Paul calls the same Spirit, first, the Spirit of Christ, and then the Spirit of him that raised up Christ from the dead.

This fact can be a strengthener of our faith, although it is hard to understand. The oneness of the Father and Son is the more obvious from this fact — they have one Spirit. So for this reason, the Spirit cannot be something different from the Father and the Son. While each person of the Trinity has his own distinct personality, each is also the whole Godhead. Thus Christ could say: "I am in the Father and the Father in me".

Let us, then, be sure of this ground of our faith. We believe in one God. By this one God, we mean a single and undivided being in whom are three persons. When we use the name God indefinitely, we also include the Son and the Spirit. But, because there is a definite order in the persons of the Godhead, we sometimes use the name God to mean the Father when we are also speaking of the Son or the Spirit as compared with the Father — e.g. the Son of God. We believe in the unity of God, the order of the persons of the Godhead, and do not detract from the Godhead of the Son and of the Spirit.

Section 14. Nothing that God created may be given honour due to him alone.

The story of the creation is told in scripture so that we of the church will seek no other god. We may not worship angels, devils, or God's creation on earth. God is greater than the things he made.

Angels. These are among God's most glorious creations. However, they are not divine beings. Let us accept the fact that God has not seen fit to give us much information about angels. We do not know when they were created. We only know from Moses that: "The heavens and earth were finished, and all their host". We do not know how many angels there are, but we know, with Elisha: "More are they that are for us than they that are against us".

From the scripture we know that angels are God's servants, made by him. They obey him and carry out his decrees. This is what "angel" means — messenger. They are called the heavenly host or army, because they surround their monarch, displaying his majesty and stand ready to obey his orders. We are comforted to know that the angels are there to serve — there to bring God's gifts to us. We are told that they watch for our safety, defend us, guide us and watch to guard us against all hurt. It may be that an angel takes care of each believer. But it is most certain that all are concerned for our safety. They rejoice in heaven over one sinner who repents, more than over ninety-nine just persons who do not need repentance.

But God has not made the angels to share his glory. He does *not* offer their help for us to trust even partly in them. Angels are God's servants. Their job is to minister his power and goodness to us.

Devils. We must realise that devils were made by God. They could not have an existence apart from him, as this would mean they had existence in themselves. But God is the only self-existent one. All life is from him. But we must be equally sure that the wickedness of devils is not from the nature that God gave them, but their nature has been corrupted by sin.

The information about devils in the Bible is given mainly to warn us against their attacks. Satan is called the strong man armed, the prince of the power of the air, a roaring lion. All these titles should make us the more watchful and ready to fight. Peter says this clearly. He describes Satan as a roaring lion seeking whom he may devour, and then tells us to "resist, steadfast in the faith" (I Peter 5:8,9). Paul tells us to arm ourselves ready for the long and dangerous battle, for "we wrestle not against flesh and blood, but against principalities, against powers, against the rulers of the darkness of this world, against spiritual wickedness in high places" (Ephesians 6:12). We must not be lazy or afraid. We are taught to be strong, bold, and diligent, persevering to the end. And we must be aware of our own weakness and ask God for help, for the armour, the strength and the wisdom we need.

The devil is not only our enemy. He is the enemy of God. We fight for God's honour. If we want to advance the kingdom of our God, we must be continually at war with the evil spirit who tries to conquer that kingdom, even planning our own eternal ruin if he can make it possible.

There will be no truce with such an enemy. He brings error into men's minds, lies instead of truth, stirs up hatred and causes disagreement and fighting. The devil is by nature evil and depraved.

The devil's wickedness is entirely due to his own choice. Christ tells us that when the devil "speaks a lie, he speaks of his own: for he is a liar and the father of lies" (John 8:44). Christ also tells us that he "did not abide in the truth". It seems from this that he once had the truth but rejected it.

Although the devil fights against God, he could not do so without God's consent. From the book of Job we learn that Satan may not carry out his plans of violence without permission. More than this, we learn from II Thessalonians 2:9–12 that the blinding of those who do not believe is not only the work of Satan, but also the judgment of God.

God is able to control devils (or, unclean spirits) completely, according to his will, but he allows them to test believers. Believers may even be refined by the trials caused by these evil spirits. These spirits may trouble us with problems, traps and attacks of evil, but they can never crush the believer. God does not allow them to do so. Paul had this kind of conflict. He wrote: "and to keep me from being too elated by the abundance a revelations, a thorn was given me in the flesh, a messenger of Satan, to harass me, to keep me from being too elated" (II Corinthians 12:7).

I must teach against the foolish idea that devils are only evil passions within ourselves which make us do wrong. Scripture clearly denies this. Scripture speaks of devils as "unclean spirits" and as fallen "angels who left their first position". So we learn that devils are not just the thoughts in men's minds but are real and have thoughts and understanding of their own. But we also have in the Bible a comparison of the children of God and the children of the devil, which would be pointless if the children of the devil were only evil thoughts. And then we are told that devils are appointed to eternal condemnation in the fire of hell. This could certainly not be true of evil thoughts.

The physical world.   We should take delight in considering the beauties of the world God has given us. One of the first signs of faith is when we realise that all around us is God's handiwork, and wonder why he made it. Studying the story of creation will strengthen our faith. We learn that God, by the power of his Word, and his Spirit, created heaven and earth out of nothing. He made them produce created things, both animate and inanimate. He gave each object its own special nature, function and position. And since they are all subject to decay, he made a way to preserve each species by giving them the power of reproduction. Then, finally, he made mankind. He distinguished men from the rest of creation by giving them beauty of form and great abilities. He shows them as the most marvellous of his works.

This is not the place for a long discussion of the great works of God. There is no splendour or style of words which will be enough to show how far beyond our understanding are his wisdom, power, righteousness and goodness as they appear in the universe. But this does not mean we should not consider them. The beauties of the universe are a mirror of God's goodness, wisdom and power. To consider creation will make our appreciation of God's greatness grow with wonder.

Let us firstly, then, marvel at the greatness of the architect who has placed the stars in position with such grandeur, fixing some in place and giving others a moving, orderly course. He controls their movement so that they measure day and night, months, years and ages. He even varies the length of the day and yet with no confusion. There are many, many examples that we could choose to show forth God's goodness and wisdom in his creation of all things, both great and small.

Secondly, let us see how this creation must have its effect on us. When by faith we see that God has designed all things for our good, we will learn to turn to him in confidence, prayer, praise and love. God could have made the world in a moment, but he spread the making of it over six days. This was a kindness and sign of his love because he thus prepared beforehand all that was needed for man. We must not be so ungrateful as to doubt the continued care of so kind a Father, who showed his care for us even before we were alive. So to think he may fail us in a time of need, when he has already showered us with so many blessings, would indeed be a sin.

Whenever we think of God as the creator of heaven and earth, let us remember that he keeps control of all his works, and that we are his children. He has guaranteed to nourish and protect us. We can confidently expect all good from him. We should ask for anything only from him and we should always thank him, because he gives us all good things. Our hearts will turn towards him so that we love and worship our Lord with all our being.

Section 15. The creation of Man.

Among all the works of God, man is the best example of his justice, wisdom and goodness. As we have already said, we can have no clear knowledge of God without a correct knowledge of ourselves. Knowledge of man includes two things: knowing how he was originally created and knowing his condition since the coming of sin (Genesis 3). Man's original state is what concerns us in this section. We must learn what man was like before he fell into sin. Then we will not blame man's wickedness on his Maker. Our faults are not from God. Neither can we blame our sins on "nature". This would be an insult to God, as it would mean there was some evil in what God had made. There are two constant facts in this subject and we may not deny either of them: there is no excuse for the sinner, and God's justice is always pure and right.

Man is made up of body and soul. By soul I mean the nobler part of him, which dwells in the body but is immortal and lives after the body has died. "Soul" and "spirit" are words that are often used interchangeably, although each has its own special meaning when used together.

Mankind has become so much concerned with material things that many people forget they have a soul. They forget, or ignore, the fact that they will have an existence after death. But they cannot live entirely without some sense of their immortality. Each man has a conscience which responds to God's moral law and can tell the difference between good and evil. Conscience is not just a mental recognition of good or evil. Neither is it just will-power. Both physical brain and will are going to die with us, and need not fear God's judgment. Yet it is true that we do feel dread of judgment and punishment if we do wrong. The conscience is a part of the *immortal* soul. Our soul is the part of us that fears to do wrong in this life because of judgment and punishment in the afterlife.

Further proof that we have a soul is seen in the excellence of the human mind. Our understanding is far above that of animals. We can think of heaven and earth. We can think about the past and look forward to the future, and have thoughts of an invisible God. Something much more than the physical body certainly goes into the making of a man.

The scriptures make it clear that the soul has an existence apart from the body. They teach us that we "dwell in houses of clay", that at death we "put off this corruptible" flesh and that at the last day we shall "receive a reward for the things done in the body". From these passages and many others we learn that the soul is distinguished from the body, and is even the main part of a man.

Some more scriptures will strengthen this teaching. Paul calls on his readers to cleanse themselves from all defilement of the flesh and the spirit (I Corinthians 7:1), showing that evil defiles the two parts of man. Peter calls Christ the Shepherd and Bishop of souls. This would be nonsense if there were no souls for Christ to take care of. It would also be nonsense for him to write about the eternal salvation of souls if human beings did not have souls. Christ makes it very plain that we have souls, when he says that we should fear him who, after death has killed the body, has power to cast the soul into hell. Christ also speaks of a soul separate from the body when he tells the story of the soul of Lazarus resting in Abraham's bosom while the soul of the rich man was in torment. This truth is affirmed by Paul. He tells us that we are absent from the Lord while we are in this body, but enjoy his presence when we leave the body.

When we consider the fact that man was made in the image of God, we will believe even more firmly that man has a soul. The glory of God does shine forth to some extent in the physical body. There is often a grace of form that cannot be denied, and it has a beauty above that of animals. But it is in the soul that we have the divine image. Adam was given a right understanding, with affections that were governed by sound reason, and senses that were under perfect and orderly control.

Mankind has largely lost this image of God in his soul, since the time when Adam sinned. Christ, the second Adam, is able to restore in us this image of himself. Paul writes to Christians who "have put on the new nature, which is being renewed in knowledge after the image of its creator" (Colossians 3:10). Now we can discover the features of this renewal. The first is knowledge. The second is righteousness or true holiness. Through the fall of Adam, man lost the light of knowledge to fill his mind and also uprightness of heart and soundness of all his faculties. We learn from II Corinthians 3:18 that we need to be changed into the image of God: "and we all, with unveiled face, beholding the glory of the Lord, are being changed into his likeness from one degree of glory to another". We are being changed into the likeness of Christ, who is the perfect image of God. His image is true holiness, purity and understanding. His image in us will reach its full splendour when we arrive in heaven.

The soul of man animates all parts of his body and takes the lead in controlling a man's life. Many philosophers have thought man was controlled by his reason, and that reason alone would lead him to do right. They did not consider that man's nature had been corrupted by the fall. They confused two states of man that are entirely different: the state of man as God created him, and his state since he has fallen.

For further information on the soul, let us accept this, then. The human soul has two parts: the understanding and the will. The work of understanding is to tell the difference between good and evil. The work of the will is to choose between the two.

God created man with a will that was free. Adam had the power to resist temptation if he had willed to do so. And Adam fell by his own will. His mind and will were perfect, in the original state in which he was created, and all his parts were in submission to his will. He was free to choose good or evil. But when he chose evil, he ruined himself and so corrupted all his faculties. From that time on, man has not been completely controlled by reason. The philosophers were right in thinking that man would not be a reasoning creature unless he was free to choose between good and evil. They saw that if he did not control his life by his own will, there would be no goodness in choosing good nor badness in choosing evil. But they are not completely right. We must take into account the change in human nature. Man no longer has a free will. Our wills are bound by sin.

Section 16. God continues to govern every part of his universe.

We believe that God did not merely create the universe and then leave it to run its own course. This is one of the main points of difference between Christians and unbelievers. We recognise the work of God in the continuous course of nature as much as we do in its origin. Many people are convinced that there is a creator God when they see his work, but it requires faith in the heart to see his continued work. "Through faith we understand that the world was created by the word of God" (Hebrews 11:3).

We must, however, go on to believe in God's providence, or care of the present world. We must learn not only that God is the creator of all things, but also that he is governor and preserver and that he specially cares for and cherishes every one of his creatures, even the smallest sparrow.

We must clearly see that the providence of God has nothing to do with fortune or chance. For hundreds of years and even in our own time, men have thought many happenings were by chance. If a man was attacked by robbers, shipwrecked at sea, found an oasis in a desert or had a hairbreadth escape from death, it was all ascribed to chance. But we know that even the hairs of our head are numbered. We know that the One who cares for us does

44

not allow anything to happen to us just by chance. All events are controlled by the secret counsel of God.

Remember, then, that God has omnipotence (all-power), which is not the omnipotence that the philosophers think he has. God is not idle now that he has completed creation. He is watchful, powerful, always working. He is all-powerful not because he set the world going, but because he governs heaven and earth with his kindly care. And this does not mean, merely, that he has set in order the course of nature. His goodness continues in fatherly love to all his people.

When we fully recognise God's omnipotence, we will both obey him and rest secure in his protection. We will have no superstitious fears. Some people think the stars govern the world, and worry about horoscopes. We can rest assured that the world is completely governed by the secret will of God, so that nothing happens without his permission, knowledge and will.

Another point that we must have clear in our minds is that God's care is much more than foreknowledge. His care is shown in continued action. To say that God governs the world in general without controlling each individual person, is not true. The human being does not move or act by accident, nor by his own free will. God's care in the world today means that he continues to work in the affairs of men. The decision about what occurs in the world is not partly God's choice and partly man's — the choice is always God's.

God controls both animate and inanimate things. By his fatherly care we have a good harvest or a bad one, a safe voyage or a shipwreck. God is all-powerful. We must realise that it is by his decision that we have good times or bad. We know that he is so kind as to provide the good things we need. And when we go through bad times, we must not think that is because he could not provide anything better for us. Christ has proclaimed as a universal truth that not even so small a creature as a sparrow falls to the ground without the will of the Father in heaven.

We know that God made the world for man. We must expect that he governs it for the benefit of man. The prophet Jeremiah exclaims: "I know, O Lord, that the way of man is not in himself, that it is not in man who walks to direct his steps" (Jeremiah 10:23). Solomon tells us: "A man's steps are ordered by the LORD; how then can man understand his way?" Because of these verses we cannot hold the teaching of some people that God gives man the power to move while man chooses his own movements. The choice and purpose is God's, all the way. Even happenings that we may think are more by chance than others, are controlled by God. If one man is accidentally killed by another, it is not without God's permission. "If he did not lie in wait for him, but God let him fall into his hand ..." (Exodus 21:13). Many of us think the casting of lots is an appeal to chance alone, but God claims his control of this too: "The lot is cast into the lap, but the decision is wholly from the Lord" (Proverbs 16:33).

God's loving care over the world is not only general. It is particular. There are many examples in the Bible of his loving care in special cases. He sent a wind to bring quails from the sea (Numbers 11:31). He made a storm when he wanted Jonah to be thrown into the sea. The Bible tells us of his control over all nature. "Who makest the clouds thy chariot ... ridest on the wings of the wind, who makest the winds thy messengers, fire and flame thy ministers" (Psalm 104:3,4). "He commanded and raised the stormy wind, which lifted up the waves of the sea ... He made the storm be still, and the waves of the sea were hushed" (Psalm 107:25,29). Even such an ordinary thing as the bread we eat is given by God who asks us to pray to him for it: "Give us this day our daily bread".

The teaching that God controls every part of his world all the time can be made to sound horrible, by making it seem as if the world is controlled by "fate". This idea must be rejected by the Christian. "Fate" is similar to "blind chance" or "fortune", and this is NOT what we teach. The idea of fate controlling mankind is completely non-Christian. We believe our loving God watches over everything with fatherly care.

Often, however, our minds are too dull to reach to the heights of understanding God's actions. Though all things are ordered by God's sure will, to us they appear to happen by chance. The purpose of many happenings is hidden from us.

In the story of David, there is a remarkable incident showing God's direction of events over which David had no control. At the very moment when David was surrounded by Saul in the desert of Maon, the Philisitines invaded the land, and Saul had to stop trying to capture David and go off to fight them. This incident did not happen by chance. The time was all fixed by God. If we have faith, we will be able to see that what looks to us like chance is the secret working of God's power.

Section 17. How we should use this doctrine of God's care.

We can rightly consider God's continued care and intervention in the world only if we remember that we are discussing our Maker, the Creator of the world. We must speak reverently and humbly. Many people are unwilling to think that God has more power than their own reason can understand. But we say with Paul: "O, the depth of the riches both of the wisdom and knowledge of God! How unsearchable are his judgments, and his ways past finding

47

out!" (Romans 11:33). There are mysteries which we cannot understand, but God has allowed us to know some of his ways. "The secret things belong to the Lord our God; but the things that are revealed belong to us and to our children for ever, that we may do all the words of this law" (Deuteronomy 29:29).

Comfort for Christians. However much the causes of events may be hidden from us, we can firmly believe that God is working out his plan. We can say with David: "Many, O Lord my God, are thy wonderful works which thou hast done, and thy thoughts which are toward us. They cannot be reckoned up in order unto thee: if I would declare and speak of them, they are more than can be numbered" (Psalm 40:5).

When we are in trouble, we are right to look within ourselves to see if we are the cause of our troubles. If we have sinned, we need to repent. But the heavenly Father has a right to do whatever he wills. The affliction of a man may be for punishment, but sometimes a man may endure suffering in order to show the glory of God. This was so with the man born blind. Jesus said: "Neither has this man sinned, nor his parents, but that the works of God might be made manifest in him" (John 9:3). Our human understanding considers this unfair. It is one of the mysteries we cannot grasp. We are not permitted to call God to account. We may, and must, reverence his secret counsels.

The future. From Solomon we learn that man's planning works in harmony with God. "A man's mind plans his way, but the LORD directs his steps" (Proverbs 16:9). God's decrees do not prevent us from exercising forethought and planning our affairs. But we must still acknowledge his overruling care. God gave us life and gave

48

us the means to take care of our life. He has given us some ability to foresee dangers. He has taught us to be careful and to try to remedy what is wrong. So God expects us to care for our own life. He allows us to be forewarned of danger, so we must not run into it.

Some people, looking only at the naked doctrine of God's continued intervention, draw wrong conclusions. They ask why God should punish a murderer if he killed a man who must have reached the limit of the time given him by God. But the murderer acted contrary to the plain word of God, Thou shalt not kill. God's will declared by his word is what we must obey. That God knows how to make good use of bad deeds does not make the deeds less bad.

Second causes.   In the first place, all happenings are a result of God's working. But second causes do have their place. A godly man will consider someone who does him a kindness as an agent employed by God's goodness. But he will also feel heartily grateful to the agent and try to show his gratitude. If one committed to his care died of disease because of his carelessness, he would consider himself guilty, though he knows the length of life is fixed by God's appointment. A godly man who rightly understands God's care and intervention will not abuse this teaching of God's goodness nor make excuses for sin.

Promises for Christians.   There are many promises that God will always watch over our safety. Here are some of them. "Cast your burden on the Lord, and he will sustain you; he will never permit the righteous to be moved" (Psalm 55:22). "He cares for you" (I Peter 5:9). "He who dwells in the secret place of the Most High, shall abide under the shadow of the Almighty" (Psalm 91:1). "Can a woman forget her sucking child, that she should have no compassion on the son of her womb? Even these may

49

forget, yet I will not forget you" (Isaiah 49:15).

To know such truths makes us thankful in times of prosperity; patient in times of difficulty; and marvellously confident of our future safety. We believe that prosperity comes to us through God's goodness, even if it reaches us by man. When men show us kindness, we know that God has turned their hearts to help us. When troubles come, we know that God has given them to produce in us patience and submission with quietness of mind. Remember how Joseph was so badly treated by his brothers. He did not think about their treachery, but remembered that God was working. "As for you, you meant evil against me; but God meant it for good, to bring it about that many people should be kept alive, as they are today" (Genesis 45:8; 50:21).

Does God change his mind? Some passages in the Bible seem to show that this happens. "It repented God that he had made man" (Genesis 6:6). "If that nation, against whom I have pronounced, turn from their evil, I will repent of the evil that I thought to do unto them" (Jeremiah 18:8). Sometimes his decrees were cancelled. Jonah was instructed to tell the people of Nineveh that their city would be destroyed, and then God spared it. King Hezekiah was told he would soon die, but then God gave him fifteen years more.

To repent actually means that the person who changes his mind must have been ignorant, or wrong, or weak. We cannot say that God repented in this sense, for this would mean that he did not know, or purposely did evil, or was unable to prevent evil. If repentance means only this, then the Bible denies that God can repent. "The glory of Israel will not lie or repent; for he is not a man, that he should repent" (I Samuel 15:29).

The passages above that seem to mean that God changed

his mind must be understood to be human ways of speaking. God's lofty attributes are far above our human minds. But God has described himself in a way that we can understand. His purpose, his will and his mind never change. God did not wish to overthrow Nineveh, but he did plan that the people of that city should repent because of Jonah's preaching. God did not plan to end King Hozekiah's life immediately, but God wanted Hezekiah to turn again to himself. The Lord had threatened in order to awaken men to repentance. Isaiah sent out a challenge in his time and it remains unanswered today: "For the Lord of hosts has purposed, and who will annul it? His hand is stretched out and who will turn it back?" (Isaiah 14:27).

Section 18.   God's righteous use of wicked agents.

The parts of scripture that say Satan and all wicked people are controlled by the will of God are very difficult to understand. We begin to think that God is to blame when evil is done.

Some people have tried to solve this problem by saying that some things God *does,* and some others he *permits.* But we know from the book of Job that God actually did the things that happened to Job. After Satan and the Sabeans had robbed him, Job says: "The Lord gave, and the Lord has taken away". Again, we know the Jews wanted to destroy Christ. It was also God's will that Christ should die. The disciples said this afterwards: "In this city there were gathered together against thy holy servant Jesus, whom thou didst anoint, both Herod and Pontius Pilate, with the Gentiles and the people of Israel, to do whatever thy hand and thy plan had predestined to take place" (Acts 4:27,28).

Solomon tells us that it is God who turns the mind of a

king. The fact that God controls our minds is clearly stated in the New Testament too, where it frequently says that God hardened their hearts or blinded their eyes. Romans 11:8 says: "God gave them a spirit of stupor, eyes that should not see and ears that should not hear, down to this very day".

We must not say that God should not do this. We cannot judge our maker. It would also be wrong to say there is a mistake in the Bible. Nor can we avoid this difficulty by saying we cannot understand. God has told us this is how he works and we must accept what he says.

Some people suggest that God must disagree with himself. They say he must want one thing — the good thing — and yet cause the evil to happen. But God has only one will, although it may appear divided to us. A saying of Augustine may help us to understand this: "Some men have good wishes which are not according to God's will, and others have bad wishes which are according to God's will. For instance, a good son may rightly wish that his father should live, while it is God's will that he should die; and a bad son may wickedly wish that his father should die, when it is also God's will that the father should die. And yet the godly son pleases God by wishing what God willeth not; while the wicked son displeases God by wishing what God wills".

God sometimes fulfils his own righteous purposes by means of the evil purposes of the wicked. God would not allow evil to be done, unless he, as the omnipotent God, were able to bring good out of it. Christ was crucified by God's appointment, even though the action was done by wicked men. But without this death, we could not have salvation.

Other people object to this teaching and say that if God uses wicked people, even governs their plans, he must be committing their crimes. So people must then be punished

52

merely for obeying God's orders. But this reasoning is wrong. God's commandments must always be obeyed. A person who deliberately breaks a commandment deserves punishment. God's commands are unalterable. God's will is also unalterable. The difficulty comes when it seems that God has willed something that is contrary to his commandments. In this case, perhaps we do not understand the purpose of what he wills. His will may include someone doing a wicked act, but that act is still wicked. God willed that David's adultery should be avenged by Absalom's incest; but it does not follow that God commanded Absalom to commit incest. A wicked man is still guilty, even though he may act in accordance with God's plan, because it was his own wish to act wickedly.

PART II:

THE KNOWLEDGE OF GOD THE REDEEMER.

Section 1. The fall of Adam and original sin.

Popular philosophy emphasises the dignity and mental ability of mankind. This theory flatters men by making them think that they are skilful, intelligent and wise. People are thus encouraged to produce from within themselves a desire to do good and avoid evil and to seek a good reputation. This theory tells us that there is nothing wrong in human nature.

The teaching of the Bible about the nature of man is completely different. Here we learn that God did indeed make mankind pure and good, even noble, of nature. But when we remember this, it should humble us; not make us proud. For now it is impossible to describe mankind as always pure, good and noble. When Adam disobeyed God and ate the fruit that was forbidden he polluted the whole of mankind. Now we are corrupted and unable to choose good.

God forbade Adam to eat from the tree of knowledge of good and evil, to test his obedience. If Adam obeyed, it would show that he was willingly subject to God's authority. So when Adam ate the fruit it was not just a small offence. He showed that he was not willing to recognise God as his master.

A chain of wrong thoughts led to Adam's disobedience.

The deception of Eve by the serpent led her to disbelieve the word of God and then to disobey it. The main cause of the sin was disobedience. Paul tells us that "by one man's disobedience many were made sinners" (Romans 5:19). We must also notice that Adam rebelled against the government of God by despising the truth and believing a lie.

Adam brought a curse on all creation. His sin is passed on to all his descendants. This is the doctrine of inherited corruption, which is also called original sin. Our nature, which was at first made good and pure, is now corrupt. We are affected right from our birth. David was like other men but he wrote: "Behold, I was brought forth in iniquity, and in sin did my mother conceive me" (Psalm 51:5). We are all unclean in the sight of God, even before we are born.

Paul makes this clear in Romans 5:12: "Therefore as sin came into the world through one man and death through sin, and so death spread to all men because all men sinned ...."; so by the grace of Christ righteousness and life are restored to us. Adam's sin spreads to all mankind; but Christ's salvation (by communicating righteousness) spreads to mankind to provide the remedy for sin.

Let us define original sin. Original sin is the inherited corruption of our nature, extending to every part of our soul, which first makes us deserve the wrath of God and secondly makes us do wrong things. We are so corrupted by this sin in our nature that we are condemned before God. We cannot claim that we are being condemned for another man's fault and that we ourselves are innocent. The corruption of sin is actually in us. Since we have sin in us, we deserve to be punished. The third chapter of Romans tells us very definitely about original sin.

Section 2. Man's will is in slavery.

We have learnt that sin has power over mankind in general and also over every person. We will now consider whether man has any freedom at all.

There are two dangers to avoid in discussing this. We must not think that man has lost all sense of right. This would give us an excuse for such a sin as laziness. And even worse, a man could say that he has no power to do right and therefore there is no need for him to try. The other error to avoid is that we must not claim one atom of righteousness for ourselves. If we said that we were able in ourselves to do good, we would be robbing God of his honour and would also place ourselves in danger of falling into sin through being proud.

The true situation is that we have lost all goodness. But we must learn to seek earnestly from God the goodness we do not have in ourselves and also the freedom we have lost.

Philosophers say that man's power of reason is sufficient to govern his mind and therefore his actions. They say that the will may be tempted by our senses, but remains free to choose in agreement with our reason. Even many Christian writers are in some error here. They describe the will as free, even though they see only a very limited freedom. They say man chooses willingly to do wrong and is not forced to do so. This is true, but it is a very poor freedom if it is only a freedom to do, or not to do, evil. We would have no freedom to do good.

Scripture teaches that man has no freedom to choose the good until the Holy Spirit gives him freedom. We must have a very low opinion of our own goodness and a very high opinion of the goodness that God can give us. The thought that we have goodness of our own must be rejected, for that thought comes from Satan. He is a liar, for he said to Adam and Eve: "You will be like God, knowing good and evil".

57

Many verses in the Bible emphasise that we must not think we have any goodness of our own but must turn to God. "Cursed be the man who trusts in man ... whose heart turns away from the Lord" (Jeremiah 17:5). "God delights not in the strength of the horse, nor does he have pleasure in the legs of a man; but the LORD takes pleasure in those who fear him, in those who hope in his steadfast love" (Psalm 147:10,11). "He gives power to the faint, and to him who has no might he increases strength" (Isaiah 40:29).

But God does not give his power to those who are proud or ungrateful. He waits till we see the need for strength from him. When we thirst for him, he will quench our thirst. "For I will pour water on the thirsty land and streams on the dry ground" (Isaiah 44:3). We must never think that we can do any good ourselves. We must be humble enough to ask for God's Spirit to help us. Someone once asked Augustine what the most important requirement is for a true Christian. He answered: "First, humility; secondly, humility; thirdly, humility".

When Adam sinned and caused the fall of mankind, mankind entirely lost some of God's gifts. Other gifts were spoiled but not lost. We lost the ability to love God, the ability to love our neighbour, and the desire for holiness and righteousness. We marred the gifts of soundness of mind and the desire to be morally upright.

Man has certainly not lost the power to reason. He can understand and judge and he knows the difference between good and evil. But there is a difference between understanding matters that concern our life on earth and understanding heavenly matters. We can know earthly things with our partially spoiled minds. We cannot use such corrupted minds to have any knowledge of God, of his righteousness, or of the mysteries of the kingdom of heaven.

There are very strong proofs in the world around us that man has still an ability to reason. Firstly we can see that man is a sociable creature and lives in groups. And every man reasons that there must be laws on which to base a society. Secondly, almost every person has some skill, art or aptitude. This fact shows some strong ability in the human mind. And thirdly, writers have produced such excellent works that we must certainly see in them a most able reasoning.

Although these people may not realise it, the gifts they have and the gifts that any of us have, are from the Spirit of God. He is the only source of truth.

We may wonder how much power human reason has to help us know God and understand his fatherly love toward us. The answer is that even the most clever men know very, very little if God has not given them light. The light they possess is similar to the light they may receive from one flash of lightning on a dark night. They know a little of God's attributes. They cannot plead complete ignorance as an excuse for ungodliness. But the light they have is not enough for them to reach the truth.

We learn this fact from the Bible as well as from our observation of mankind. When Peter realised that Jesus was the Christ, the Son of the living God, Jesus replied: "Flesh and blood has not revealed this to you, but my Father who is in heaven" (Matthew 16:17). Psalm 36:9 tell us: "With thee is the fountain of life. In thy light we see light". When Moses reproved the people of Israel for forgetting God's works, he said: "You have seen all that the Lord did before your eyes ... the signs, and those great wonders; but to this day the LORD has not given you a mind to understand, or eyes to see, or ears to hear" (Deuteronomy 29:2–4). The Lord speaks through Jeremiah: "I will give them a heart to know me" (Jeremiah 24:7). Of course, this means that the people did not have spiritual wisdom, but that God would give it. This is clearly stated in John 6:44: 'No one can come to me unless the Father who sent me draws him".

The apostle Paul pronounces all human wisdom to be folly (I Corinthians 1:18). Then he says: "The natural man does not receive the things of the Spirit of God, for they are folly to him and he is not able to understand them because they are spiritually discerned" (I Corinthians 2:14). The possession of spiritual understanding is the gift of God alone. This is shown in Paul's prayer: "That the God of our Lord Jesus Christ, the Father of glory, may give you a spirit of wisdom and of revelation in the knowledge of him" (Ephesians 1:17). Paul continues with: "having the eyes of your understanding enlightened" (Ephesians 1:18). Most surely, we are blind and know almost nothing of God unless he graciously enlightens us.

We may wonder whether man has knowledge about the standards God wants in our lives. Yes, we do have knowledge of right and wrong. "When the Gentiles who have not the law do by nature what the laws requires, they are a law to themselves, even though they do not have the law. They show that what the law requires is written on their hearts" (Romans 2:14,15). If Gentiles have the law written on their hearts, they certainly have some knowledge of right and wrong. Their own conscience is their law, but it does not do them very much good. They may know right from wrong; but when they continue in sin their knowledge makes them responsible and leads on to their just condemnation.

The mind of man has no power to do good. It does not even try to do good. When Paul says that he now desires to do good but cannot (Romans 7:15), he is speaking as a Christian. The natural man does not have this conflict. The natural man does not even desire to do good. Paul says that no good thing dwells in him, that is, in his flesh. Any good there is in him now comes from God and not from himself.

Only the born again man has the conflict within himself described in Romans 7:22,23: "I delight in the law of God after the inward man; but I see another law in my members, warring against the law of my mind". Augustine said: "Confess that whatsoever good you have in you is of God; whatsoever evil, of yourself. Nothing is our own, but sin".

Section 3. The will of man is in bondage to sin, and can only be set free by grace.

Jesus says: "That which is born of the flesh is flesh". The "flesh" meant here is "human nature". Paul says that the natural mind is death because it is against God (Romans 8:6–7). It is not subject to the law of God; in fact, it cannot be. The natural mind fights against God with all its powers. If this is what flesh is like, it is worthy only of death.

The Lord's argument goes further. He says that we must be born again. And "new birth" means not only a renewal of man's emotions and fleshly desires, but also of his soul. This is shown in Ephesians 4:22,23: "Put off your old nature which belongs to your former manner of life, and is corrupt through deceitful lusts, and be renewed in the spirit of your minds". Evil passions are not only from evil desires — they are from the mind.

We should have no illusions that the human mind is somehow naturally good. Jeremiah condemns it with these words: "The heart is deceitful above all things, and desperately wicked". Paul finds the same information in the prophets: "There is none righteous, no not one; no one understands, no one seeks for God. All have turned aside, together they have gone wrong; no one does good, not even one" (Romans 3:10–12).

Paul has clearly taught and shown that it is not just bad

men who have no righteousness at all. Nobody at all is righteous in his own right, except for Christ. We will never find true goodness in ourselves, even if only a few vices appear in any one man's life.

There have been men, I admit, who have tried all their lives to do good. Their constant striving to do good has been proof of a certain amount of purity. They make us think that human nature is not altogether corrupt. In these men the Lord has restrained the corrupt nature from breaking out. Such virtues are not usual to human nature. They are favours from God. But these people are still lacking in the main element of righteousness, for the first duty of man is to promote the glory of God.

The will of man is so strongly bound by sin that it cannot move towards good and would find it even harder to cling to good. Man's will is a slave to sin. If we make one movement towards God, this is entirely by God's grace. Jeremiah says: "Turn thou me and I shall be turned" (Jeremiah 31:18). Yet, man still possesses a will. When mankind fell into sin, man was placed under the need to serve sin. His will was not taken away but it became diseased. Mankind has the faculty of will. The will to do evil belongs to our corrupted nature. The will to do good is given by God's grace.

Mankind's will has lost its freedom, and must of necessity do evil. This is a hard statement to accept. We must distinguish between necessity and compulsion. Let us consider an example. We all agree that it is the nature of God that he is of necessity good. His own infinite goodness makes it impossible for him to do evil. Yet God retains the freedom of his will in exercising goodness. In the same way, although man is under a necessity to commit sin, he is not compelled to sin. People sin willingly. The mind of a man turns eagerly towards sin, not because he is violently forced, but because of his own desire.

Grace alone heals the corruption of human nature. The grace of God working in us even starts in us the desire for righteousness. Then this grace continues and strengthens this desire so that we will persevere to the end. Paul writes: "I am sure that he who began a good work in you will bring it to completion at the day of Jesus Christ" (Philippians 1:6). God changes our will. He does not just assist a weak will. The Bible shows in the following passage that human will is so worthless that it must be transformed by God: "A new heart also will I give you, and a new spirit will I put within you; and I will take away the stony heart out of your flesh, and I will give you a heart of flesh. And I will put my Spirit within you, and cause you to walk in my statutes, and ye shall keep my judgments, and do them" (Ezekial 36:26,27). The human will is not abolished, but made new by being changed from evil to good. "For God is in you both to will and to work for his good pleasure" (Philippians 2:13).

After the human will is converted solely by the power of God, God continues working good in us. We still have no share in performing good works, but have to rely on him to work through us. God claims for himself everything that is good and right in the will of man. "I will give them one heart and one way, that they may fear me for ever ... I will not turn away from doing good to them; and I will put the fear of me in their hearts, that they may not turn from me".

Both David and Solomon realised that they needed God to lead them into good. "The Lord our God be with us, that he may incline our hearts unto him, to walk in all his ways and to keep his commandments" (I Kings 8:58). David asks God: "Create in me a clean heart, O God, and put a new and right spirit within me" (Psalm 51:10). He saw that he could only have purity from God.

Christ taught this truth even more definitely: "As the branch cannot bear fruit by itself, unless it abides in the vine, neither can you, unless you abide in me. I am the vine, you are the branches. He who abides in me, and I in him, he it is that bears much fruit" (John 15:4). Equally decisive is Christ's conclusion: "without me you can do nothing" (John 15:5).

Paul wrote: "God is at work in you, both to will and to work for his good pleasure" (Philippians 2:13). The first cause of a good work is the will to do it. The second is an effective effort to accomplish it. The author of both willing and working good in us is God. We steal from God whenever we claim for ourselves either the will or the deed. God begins and God finishes.

In the experience of conversion, God does not give a man a choice whether to obey or disobey. A renewed will is given by God's choice, not because man chooses to ask for it. The Lord, by his Spirit, directs, bends, regulates our heart, and reigns in it as in his own kingdom.

Now that it has been proved that it does not depend on man to accept or reject the grace of God, another truth arises from this established truth. A person will persevere in the Christian life after God has chosen him. This perseverance is the gift of God and is not the reward of human merit.

The way grace works is not to take away man's will, but to change it from a bad will to a good will, and then afterwards to assist it by changing the man's impulses so that he obeys from the heart. Grace is not given to all men. Those who receive it, do not receive it as a reward for their merits or works, but as a free favour. The will of man does not obtain grace by freedom, but freedom by grace.

Section 4. How God works in the hearts of men.

The human will is a little like a horse. It may have either

God or the devil as rider. When God is the rider, he turns us toward the right way. If the devil is the rider, our direction is toward disaster. The natural man is not compelled, reluctantly, to obey the devil, but he is so bewitched by the devil's cleverness that he necessarily yields and obeys willingly.

In the book of Job one action is described as the work of God, of the devil and of men. How can this be true? The Chaldeans killed his shepherds and stole his sheep. There were three different purposes in this act. The Lord wanted to exercise Job's patience; Satan aimed to drive him to despair; and the Chaldeans planned to enrich themselves by robbery. The plan of each fitted together. The Lord allowed Satan to afflict Job and to use the Chaldeans as his instruments. Satan stirred up their minds, already corrupted, to commit the crime, so they rushed into their evil work and became guilty.

When we read in the Bible that God hardened the heart of the wicked, we cannot explain it by saying that God "foreknew" what they would do and acted accordingly, nor that he "permitted" something contrary to his real will. There are two parts to the real answer:

1. The man from whom God withdraws light is left in darkness. Without God's Spirit a man's heart is as hard as stone. So it is true to say that God hardened the heart.
2. God carries out judgments by using Satan, and it is Satan who indirectly controls the will of wicked people.

When we look around, we easily think that man has control of his own destiny, but the Bible shows us that man's will is controlled by God. God persuaded the Egyptians to give the people of Israel their most precious treasures just before the Israelites left (Exodus 12:35,36). Jacob knew that it is God who changes men's minds according to his own plan, when he said to his sons: "May God Almighty grant you mercy before the man" (Genesis 43:14).

Section 5. Answers to arguments that man has a free will.

1. People say that if man sins of necessity, it is not really sin. It can only be sin if man has a will free to avoid sinning.

Sin cannot be excused by saying it is necessary. Neither can we say that sin can be avoided because it is voluntary. Sin is by no means excusable when we remember that the will of man is subject to sin, not because of the way our wills were created, but because our wills have been corrupted. Adam of his own accord submitted to the devil, and mankind is bound by sin ever since.

The second part of the argument confuses willingness with freedom. I have already shown that things may be done willingly by those who have no freedom of choice between good and evil.

2. If man cannot choose good or bad, people say it is not fair to punish or reward him.

We reply that it is quite just of God to punish sin since the sinner is to blame. He sins willingly so it does not matter whether he sins with a mind free or enslaved. As for rewards, we owe them to the kindness of God; not to any merit of our own. If we get what we deserve, we will get punishment. But God bestows — not the deserved punishment — but undeserved grace.

3. Some say that a man must have power to obey or we could not exhort or warn him.

But it was Christ who said: "Without me you can do nothing", and yet he reproves evil deeds and exhorts to good works. Paul reproves the Corinthians for lack of love, and yet prays earnestly that the Lord will give them love.

Exhortations are of use in two ways: first, at the judgment seat of Christ they will serve as a witness against those who have rejected them. Such people must blame themselves for their hardness. But secondly, exhortations are of great use to believers. God uses his Word to prepare us to receive the grace that will be needed to obey his exhortation. And exhortations are of course useful to convict a man of sin. They encourage us to desire what is good, arouse us from laziness and make us hate sin.

4.   Some argue that, either God is mocking us when he demands holiness and forbids sin; or else, we *do* have the power to give what he asks.

This common error arises from utter ignorance of the nature of the law. The writings of Paul make it clear that, although we cannot keep the law, it was given to convince us of our sin. "The law was added because of transgressions"; "by the law is the knowledge of sin"; "I had not known sin but by the law"; "the law entered that the offence might abound" (Galatians 3:19; Romans 3:20; 7:7; 5:20).

People are not without sense, like stones. There is some purpose in God giving his law. The ungodly at least learn from it that God hates their lusts. And the law is most certainly of use when they learn from it their inability to live righteously and run to take refuge in God's grace. Augustine said this: "God commands what we cannot give, that we may know what to ask for". God may command from us who are his, whatever he wants because he gives us what he commands!

5.   Some verses seem to indicate that man has a free will, e.g.: "Seek good and not evil, that you may live" (Amos 5:14); "If you return, O Israel, says the Lord, to me you should return" (Jeremiah 4:1).

But surely, the correct view of these verses is that God acts with justice when he tells the wicked that they will not share his favours until they depart from their wicked ways. There is sufficient reason for God to say this even if he only shows that it is fair when he excludes them from the blessings that belong to true worshippers. When God adds a promise to a command, it is to stir up our lazy natures by its sweetness.

6.   The Bible describes our good works as our own. Some men claim that if God acts through us to make us do good works, then those works are not ours.

But again I say that God does not act on a man as if he were a stone. We ascribe to man natural powers to approve, to reject, to be willing or unwilling, to co-operate or to resist. He can approve of vanity, reject real good, be willing to do wrong, be unwilling to do right, endeavour to commit wickedness, resist righteousness. But when a man's will is renewed, it is true to say that he works when the Holy Spirit works in him, for his will is then the same as that of the Spirit of God.

Section 6.   Ruined man must seek salvation in Christ.

Human beings are all in a state of corruption which can only bring them shame until they are changed by Christ the Saviour. We may learn that God is a Father, but our conscience will tell us that we are not worthy to be his sons. We can become sons through the death of Christ. "And this is life eternal, to know thee, the only true God, and Jesus Christ whom thou hast sent" (John 17:3). Nobody can become a son of God without the intervention of Christ. "But to all who received him, who believed in his name, he gave power to become children of God" (John 1:12).

Right through the Old Testament times, the people were taught to look forward to a Messiah, the Christ. Here are just two references to Christ: "Behold a virgin shall conceive, and bear a son" (Isaiah 7:14); "I will set over them one shepherd, my servant David (Christ, the descendant of David) and he shall feed them; he shall feed them and be their shepherd. And I, the Lord will be their God" (Ezekiel 34:23,24).

There never has been and never will be any saving knowledge of God except through Jesus Christ.

Section 7. The purpose of the law.

The whole Old Testament covenant, including the law, was given to encourage a desire for God. It was a picture of truth, but a temporary one. God did not really want the smell of burning fat; and the shedding of the blood of animals could not really take away sin. As early as I Samuel 15:22 the people were told: "To obey is better than sacrifice, and to listen is better than the fat of rams". Isaiah promised that all sins should be atoned for by one sacrifice (Isaiah 53:5,6). "But Christ is the end of the law, that every one who has faith may be justified" (Romans 10:4).

The moral law shows us that we are guilty before God. If we could keep it perfectly, we would receive eternal life. But the weakness of the law is seen in that no man has ever completely kept the law. Not even the greatest of saints has loved God with all his heart, and mind, and soul and strength. Solomon said: "Surely there is not a righteous man on earth who does good and never sins" (Ecclesiastes 7:20; I Kings 8:46).

There are three main purposes of the moral law. The first is that it shows the righteousness of God. By contrast, the sinfulness of man shows that man deserves to be condemned. Paul says: "If it had not been for the law, I should not have known sin; I should not have known what it is to covet if the law had not said, You shall not covet" (Romans 7:7). He had already explained (Romans 3:20) that "By the law is the knowledge of sin". The law is like a mirror to show us how weak we are and how we always tend towards sin. He explains later: "God has concluded all to be in unbelief" not that he might destroy all, or leave all to perish, but "that he might have mercy on all" (Romans 11:32).

The second purpose of the law is that it restrains men who do not care about right and wrong unless they are forced to do so. The hearts of these men are not changed, but the law holds them back from carrying out their wickedness. It is necessary for God to restrain men in this way, or else the world would become a place of never-ending fighting and confusion.

The third purpose is for the believers in whom God lives and reigns. The law helps believers daily to learn more about the nature of God and of his will, which is what they long to do. Besides this, believers need encouragement as well as teaching, and when they read and study the law of God, they will find that they are encouraged to obey, and are strengthened in their minds so that they do not so easily fall into evil ways. A believer once wrote: "The law of the Lord is perfect, reviving the soul; the testimony of the Lord is sure, making wise the simple; the precepts of the Lord are right, rejoicing the heart; the commandment of the Lord is pure, enlightening the eyes" (Psalm 19:7,8). "Thy word is a lamp to my feet and a light to my path" (Psalm 119:105).

Section 8. The moral law.

God uses the law to give us true knowledge of his righteous standards. We will worship him and think humbly of ourselves. By stating his right to command us, he calls us to worship him as he deserves, and by showing us his standard of goodness, he shows our unrighteousness and inability to do right. But we also learn that he longs for us to follow after righteousness. The fear of eternal death, which is the just reward of our unrighteousness, should make us turn to God for mercy. Then we find that he has been merciful already and drawn us towards himself with his wonderful love and sweet promises. All that we have is his so, if we give him ourselves, we only repay a debt. He has promised us the reward of blessings both in this world and in the next. To evildoers he has promised trouble in this world and eternal death in the world to come.

The law requires from us spiritual righteousness as well as outward goodness which is easily seen. The commands of an earthly king would be different. He could forbid fornication, murder or theft, but could only enforce it by taking notice of outward acts. But when God, who sees all things, forbids fornication, murder or theft, his prohibition extends to the thoughts of the heart — such as lust, hatred and covetousness.

The law (Exodus chapter 20) was purposely divided into two parts. The first part deals with a man's relationship to God, since this is the basis of all righteousness. The second part deals with a man's relationship with other men. Christ summarises the whole law in two sections: "You shall love the Lord your God with all your heart, and with all your soul, and with all your mind. This is the first and great commandment. And the second is like it, You shall love your neighbour as yourself. On these two commandments depend all the law and the prophets" (Matthew 22:37–40).

Part I of the law

First commandment: "I am the Lord your God, who brought you out of the land of Egypt, out of the house of bondage. You shall have no other gods before me".

God's claim to authority is in the word "Lord". He is the one above all, who has existence in himself and holds together everything else in existence. He encourages obedience by mentioning a great kindness he has done. Then he commands complete worship, trust, prayer and thanksgiving — all that rightly belongs to him as God. The expression "before me" shows clearly the insult which is given to the Lord by idolatry. To put an imaginary deity before God provokes him to jealousy in the way an adulterous woman would provoke her husband to jealousy by bringing her lover into his presence.

Second commandment: "You shall not make for yourself any graven image, or any likeness of anything that is in the heaven above, or that is in the earth beneath, or that is in the water under the earth; you shall not bow down to them or serve them".

He forbids us to try to show the incomprehensible God by material shapes, and forbids us to give worship to images of any kind. Our God will not allow any rival.

Third commandment: "You shall not take the name of the Lord in vain".

We are to learn from this to regard the majesty of God's name as most holy. We must always think and speak reverently about God and the divine mysteries.

Fourth commandment: "Remember the sabbath day to keep it holy".

There were three reasons for this commandment: (a) The people needed a reminder that they should stop doing their own work and allow God to work in them. (b) A day to assemble and hear the law and think on God's works. (c) A day to cease from work for their own physical benefit. In these times, we still need a day of rest and worship.

Part II of the law

First commandment: "Honour your father and mother".
 God requires us to honour our parents and also those whom God has placed in a position of ruling over us. They are to be obeyed.

Sixth commandment: "You shall not kill".
 This means not only that we must not injure another man, but we should care for the safety of others. And this includes our inward attitude too. "Whoever hates his brother is a murderer" (I John 3:5).

Seventh commandment: "You shall not commit adultery".
 The whole course of our life must be governed by the principles of chastity and clean living.

Eighth commandment: "You shall not steal".
 If we want to obey this commandment, we must be content with our situation in life. We must seek to gain nothing unless we gain it honourably and legitimately.

Ninth commandment: "You shall not bear false witness against your neighbour".
 God is truth and he hates falsehood. We too must always deal with one another completely truthfully. Neither must we harm our neighbour by slander or gossip.

Tenth commandment: "You shall not covet your neighbour's house; you shall not covet your neighbour's wife, or his manservant, or his ox, or his ass, or anything that is your neighbour's".

God forbids us to think any thought that could stir up our hearts to the evil that would make us want to injure our neighbour. Every thought and wish should agree with what is in the best interests of our neighbour.

These commandments require that man must be shaped according to the standard of the purity of God, so that we will love God and our neighbour. Christ gives a wide meaning to the word "neighbour". The parable of the Good Samaritan teaches that our neighbours are not only our fellow-countrymen, but also strangers and foreigners. Christ taught that "Whatever you wish that men would do to you, do so to them; for this is the law and the prophets" (Matthew 7:12). This was Christ's summary of the law.

Paul gives another summary that is just as demanding of our concentrated attention and effort: "For the whole law is fulfilled in one word, You shall love your neighbour as yourself" (Galatians 5:14). Christ has, of course, taught this also.

(There is one other point to make clear. Some people teach that some sins — e.g. a passing thought of covetousness — are not so bad as others and their punishment will not mean death. But we read these words in the Bible: "The wages of sin is death" (Romans 6:23). This text obviously means all sins, not just some of them. Christ taught (Matthew 5:19): "Whoever breaks one of the least of these commandments and teaches men so, shall be least in the kingdom of heaven".)

Section 9.   Christ was known in Old Testament times, but not fully revealed.

God had a purpose in instructing the people of Israel to sacrifice for sin because by this means he taught them to look forward to the coming of one who would be the final sacrifice for sin. We are told this in I Peter 1:10: "the prophets who prophesied of the grace that was to be yours searched and inquired about this salvation". Christ told the disciples: "Blessed are your eyes, for they see, and your ears, for they hear. Truly, I say to you, many prophets and righteous men longed to see what you see, and did not see it, and to hear what you hear, and did not hear it" (Matthew 13:16,17).

The promises of free forgiveness of sins found in the Old Testament look forward to the coming of the gospel in the New Testament. The gospel is "the power of God, who saved us and called us with a holy calling, not in virtue of our own works, but in virtue of his own purpose and the grace which he gave us in Christ ages ago, and now has manifested through the appearing of our Saviour Christ Jesus" (II Timothy 1:9,10). Paul tells us that in Christ, God gave what he had formerly promised.

The difference between the law of the Old Testament and the gospel of the New Testament is that the law is an agreement based on a righteousness earned by works, while the gospel is an agreement based on a righteousness received by faith without a man's works. But this does not mean the law is cancelled; in fact it is confirmed. The ceremonial law is not discounted by the work of Christ, but fulfilled. The sacrifices were a symbol of removal of sin by the shedding of blood, but when Christ died it was the actual removal of sin, not just the symbol.

Section 10. Similarities between the Old and New Testaments.

The Old and New Testament proclaim the same message. There is, however, a difference in the way the message is taught. There are three main aspects in which God's treatment of the Israelites is the same as the treatment of believers everywhere.

1. The agreement by which the Israelites were reconciled to God was not based on their own merits, but completely on the mercy of God who called them. (I will say more about this point later on).

2. The Israelites knew of Christ, the anointed one, as the mediator by whom they would receive salvation. This has already been proved (see Section 9).

3. The aim given to the Jews was the same as that given to all believers. This was not happiness and wealth in this present life, but the hope of immortality.

Paul states definitely that the gospel he preached is the one which "God had promised before time through his prophets in the holy scriptures" (Romans 1:2). He says later that the righteousness of faith taught by the gospel was "witnessed to by the law and the prophets" (Romans 3:21).

God's agreement with his people was: "I will be to you a God and you shall be to me a people" (Leviticus 26:12). If the people of Israel were to be God's people, they must share in the life he gives, in his blessedness and in his salvation. God does not mean only earthly happiness. He means that his people are to be delivered from death, and preserved by his everlasting mercy. The prophets also believed this and wrote about it under God's guidance: "The Lord is our judge, the Lord is our ruler, the Lord is our king; he will save us" (Isaiah 33:22). Yes, Isaiah knew that he could expect eternal salvation from God. Hebakkuk also knew that God gives eternal life: "Art thou not from everlasting, O Lord my God, my holy one? We shall not die" (Habakkuk 1:12).

We cannot think that the people of Israel looked only for earthly blessing when we consider the lives of some of their leaders. Abraham most certainly did not feel he had reached the best God had for him, even when he felt most blessed. "By faith Abraham sojourned in the land of promise, as in a foreign land, living in tents with Isaac and Jacob, heirs with him of the same promise. For he looked forward to the city which has foundations, whose builder and maker is God" (Hebrews 11:9,10). "These all died in faith, not having received what was promised, but having seen it and greeted it from afar, and having acknowledged that they were strangers and exiles on the earth ... They desire a better country, that is a heavenly one. Therefore God is not ashamed to be called their God, for he has prepared for them a city" (Hebrews 11:13,16).

It is certain that God promised the people of Israel not only food, pleasures, wealth and power in the present world — he also promised eternal life.

Section 11.   The differences between the Old Testament and the New Testament.

Although the Old and New Testaments are both the revelation of the grace of God, there are some differences between them. These differences are in the ways God administered his grace.

1.   In the Old Testament, God turned the thoughts of his people towards their heavenly inheritance by promising earthly blessings as a foretaste of it. Now that he has given us the gospel, we can look forward to heavenly blessings without having earthly pictures of them.

2.   In the Old Testament there are types and figures of things which are to come. The symbol of sacrifice in the temple was fulfilled when Christ died as the sacrificial lamb himself. All the earlier sacrifices were a picture of the death of Christ. So the difference is this: in the Old Testament

77

there are types and symbols, but in the New Testament these are fulfilled. Now we no longer have symbols but realities.

3. In the Old Testament the law was written on stones. It was impersonal and impossible. In the New Testament the law is personal, written within us by the Lord himself, and it is the Lord who gives us the grace to follow it (see Jeremiah 31:31–34): "I will put my law within them, and I will write it on their hearts; and I will be their God, and they shall be my people. And no longer shall each man teach his neighbour, saying: 'Know the Lord', for they shall all know me" (verses 33,34).

4. The Old Testament is a covenant (agreement) of slavery, but the New Testament is one of liberty. Paul tells us this in Romans 8:15: "For you did not receive the spirit of slavery to fall back into fear, but you have received the spirit of sonship". The law struck terror into the conscience, but the gospel in the New Testament sets the conscience free and fills the heart with joy.

5. Before the coming of Christ in the flesh, the Lord restricted his dealings to one chosen nation. In Deuteronomy 10:15 Moses explains this to the people of Israel: "Yet the Lord set his heart in love upon your fathers and chose their descendants after them, you above all peoples".

God gave to the people of Israel his covenant, many privileges and even his own presence. He treated Israel as his tenderly loved child. Other nations were treated as foreigners, shut off from approach to him. Israel was sanctified by God while the others were left in their sin.

But when Christ, the mediator between God and man, was revealed, the wall that restricted the other nations from entering into blessing was broken down. Then God proclaimed peace to people who were far away from him. From then on, there is no difference between Jew and

Gentile; members of both races are reconciled to God and grow together into one people. Christ does not just allow Gentiles to enter into his heavenly kingdom as second-rate citizens, but gives them full privileges so that it does not matter at all whether a man is Jew or Gentile. "There is neither Jew nor Greek, there is neither slave nor free, there is neither male nor female; for you are all one in Christ Jesus" (Galatians 3:28).

We may not accuse God of inconsistency because he uses one method and then another in dealing with men. Just as the farmer does one kind of work in winter and another in summer, God must work in different ways in different situations. He will have "the ends of the earth for his possession" and have "dominion from sea to sea and from the river to the ends of the earth" (Psalm 2:8; 72:8).

Section 12.   It was necessary for Christ to become man in order to be mediator.

The one who would mediate between God and man had to be both God and man.

Our sins were like a thick cloud separating us from God and keeping us out of his kingdom, so a mediator was needed who was not hindered by the cloud of sin. Man could not reach God. So God's Son became man, a sinless man, who was able to reach God and stand before him as a pure man.

Our case was hopeless. A miracle was required to bridge the gulf between our defilement and God's infinite purity; a miracle of incarnation in which the Godhead was united to our humanity.

Even if man had not sinned, his position was so low that he would not have been able to approach God, his maker. But man also has his inherited corruption and his own sin-stained life to keep him from having any right at all to enter God's presence. How wonderful that there was a man who was able to approach God to represent mankind and act as our mediator. "There is one mediator between God and men, the man Christ Jesus" (I Timothy 2:5). This sentence is further explained by a verse in Hebrews: "For we have not a high priest who is unable to sympathize with our weaknesses, but one who in every respect has been tempted as we are, yet without sinning" (Hebrews 4:15).

The work of the mediator was of an extraordinary character. He did not merely bring us into favour with God, but he brought us into God's family by making the sons of men, the sons of God. Jesus Christ, who was both Son of God and Son of man was, of course, the only one who could do this. Since he had made God's people his brothers, he could say: "I am ascending to my Father and your Father, to my God and your God" (John 20:17). Following on from this, we have the glorious fact that we shall inherit God's kingdom, because God's Son — to whom it belonged — has made us his brothers. If we are his brothers, we must also be heirs of the inheritance. "If children, then heirs; heirs of God and fellow-heirs with Christ" (Romans 8:17).

It was essential for Christ to become man because mankind was ruined by disobedience. Christ was able, as a man, to obey God, to satisfy the justice of God, and to pay the penalty of the sin of mankind. If Christ had been only God and not also man, he could not have experienced death. Yet death was the penalty for man's sin and he wanted to pay it for us. If Christ had been only man and not also God, he could not have overcome death. The answer was to take human nature into union with divine nature. Thus in his human nature Christ suffered death and in the power of his divine nature Christ battled with death and won victory over it for us.

There are yet other important reasons why it was essential for Christ to become man so that we are redeemed by one who was both God and man. Christ is the life and thus had the power to swallow up death. He is righteousness itself and thus had power to conquer sin. He is stronger than the world and stronger than the powers of the air and thus had power to conquer the powers of this world and the devil.

The men who say that Christ was merely man or only God are guilty of serious error. To say that he was only a man takes away his glory. To say that he was only God and not also man robs him of his great kindness and condescension. Teachers of such wrong doctrine are depriving men of the basis of faith, for we can have no forgiveness of sin without Christ, who was both God and man.

Section 13. Christ was truly human.

We already have clear proof that Christ was God; now we must consider that he became a man in order to be mediator.

Some people once thought that Christ's earthly body was just a vision and that he did not have a man's body at all. Others have looked at scriptures such as "made in the likeness of man", "found in fashion as a man" (Philippians 2:7,8), and thought that these indicated that Christ's flesh was not that of a man, but a heavenly body. These scriptures were being misinterpreted. Paul is not here telling us the nature of the body of Christ but showing that Christ, who had a right to display the glory of his divine nature, humbly showed himself as a man.

There are many passages in the Bible from which we may learn that Christ was truly a man. We know he was born from a virgin's womb, and came into the world in the same way as the rest of mankind. He is described as descended from man: "Son of David, son of Abraham" (Matthew 1:1), "made of the seed of David according to the flesh" (Romans 1:3). And Christ frequently described himself as Son of man.

Paul tells us that "God sent forth his Son, born of woman, born under the law, to redeem those who were under the law" (Galatians 4:4,5). The people to be redeemed were under the law. Christ had to become under the law to redeem them, so he had to become a man. The same teaching is given in Hebrews 2:14: "Since therefore the children share in flesh and blood, he himself likewise partook of the same nature, that through death he might destroy the power of death".

We learnt in Section 12 that the mediator between God and men had to be both man and God, so this is another proof that Christ was truly a man. Paul says clearly that when God sent "his own Son in the likeness of sinful flesh and for sin, he condemned sin in the flesh" (Romans 8:3). God could condemn human sin only in human flesh and so Christ became truly flesh in order to suffer that condemnation.

Some writers have objected that if Christ had really been born as a man he would have been stained with the corruption which is on the whole human race since the sin of Adam. The marvel is that Christ was not stained with sin and consequently he was able to free mankind from sin. "Then as one man's trespass led to condemnation for all men, so one man's act of righteousness leads to acquittal and life for all men" (Romans 5:18).

Section 14. The two natures in the person of the mediator.

In John 1:14 we read that the Word was made flesh. This does not mean that the Word was changed into flesh, nor that the Son of God was mixed with flesh. But it means that he chose a human body for himself as his temple or dwelling-place. His two natures were joined in such a way that he retained his whole nature as God and yet also held the whole nature of a man, while still being only one person, Christ.

It is hard to find anything on earth with which to compare this mysterious fact of two natures in one person, but one good example is man himself. A man has two distinct parts, body and soul; and yet they are put together in such a way that having a physical body does not prevent him from having a soul, nor does having a soul mean that it cannot live in a physical body. We may say of the soul things which cannot truthfully be said of the body, and we may similarly say things of the body that could not refer to the soul. Although we may speak of the different parts of a man, he is still *one* person; in the same way, Christ was one person with two natures.

We can be sure that Christ was not a mere man when we read passages such as: "The first born of every creature ... all things were created through him and for him ... and in him all things hold together" (Colossians 1:15–17), and also when Christ speaks of the glory that he had with the Father before the world existed.

We can be equally sure that Christ was not God without also being human, for there are many passages in the Bible written of him that refer to his human nature and could not be written of God. The scriptures speak of his human nature when Christ is called the Father's servant (Isaiah 42:1); and when we are told that he increased in wisdom and stature, and in favour with God and man; and that he does not know when the last day shall be or speak by his own authority.

Some passages refer to both natures at once, and this reveals the truth concerning the person of Christ even more clearly. Christ was given certain functions and titles that could only be given to a man who was much more than mere man — he was God as well. Christ was given power to forgive sins; to bestow righteousness and holiness; to judge mankind, and be honoured as the Father is honoured. He is the light of the world; the good shepherd; the only door; the true vine. Only God could do or be these things.

Section 15. Christ is our prophet, our priest and our king.

During the days of the Old Testament, God sent many prophets at many different times so that the people of Israel always had someone to teach them about God. But everyone knew that full knowledge would not be given until the Messiah came. Even the Samaritans believed this. "I know that Messiah is coming (he who is called Christ); when he comes, he will show us all things" (John 4:25). The Messiah had been promised: "Behold, I made him a witness to the peoples, a leader and commander for the peoples" (Isaiah 55:4). Now, after a long line of prophets, the great revealer had come. "In many and various ways God spoke to our fathers by the prophets; but in these last days he has spoken to us by a Son" (Hebrews 1:1,2).

Christ is also a king. His kindgom, however, is not physical, but spiritual. And because his kingdom is spiritual, it is eternal, and eternal for both the church and the individual. Christ, just before he was killed by men, said: "My kingdom is not of this world" (John 18:36).

During this life we have trials, but the knowledge of the fact that we belong to his spiritual kingdom — a kingdom that cannot be moved — should cause us to rejoice in expectation of immortality and life with him.

Christ's role as priest is vital to our salvation. We have already learnt that he is our mediator; a priest is a mediator between God and men, and this priest was able to perform his work because he was free from all taint of sin. He could reconcile us to God by his own holiness. In the Old Testament, it was against the law for the priest at the temple to attempt to approach God in the holy of holies without the blood of a sacrificed animal. This was to teach the people that without a sacrifice for sin, God could not receive them. Jesus Christ is the priest we need because he makes the sacrifice to remove our sins, make us clean in life, and obtain favour with God for us when we had lost any right to come before him because of our sin.

The unique thing in Christ's action as priest for us is that, instead of sacrificing a sheep or a bull, he sacrificed himself. This was the only way of making a sacrifice that would last forever, for he was completely sinless and yet he died for sin. Because the sacrifice he made is eternal, he can plead forever as our priest before God, and we can receive God's favour. So Christ is both the victim and the priest. No other victim could turn away God's anger at our sin; and no other person was worthy of the great honour of offering up the only-begotten Son of God. Here we must speak against an error of the Roman Catholics who claim that their priest offers Christ up again every time they celebrate mass or communion. This is completely contrary to what is taught in scripture.

The people of Israel were taught to anoint their leaders with oil as a sign that they had a special task. The name Messiah was given to the promised mediator for this means "anointed". The prophets, the priests and the kings were anointed. Christ, our Messiah, is all these — prophet, priest and king.

Section 16.   The redeeming work of Christ.

We have learnt so far that in Christ we seek deliverance, life and salvation, because we are condemned, dead and ruined. "And there is salvation in no-one else, for there is no other name under heaven given among men by which we must be saved" (Acts 4:12). The name Jesus means: "He shall save his people from their sins" (Matthew 1:21). Christ is the only way for us to find salvation.

Reconciliation.   We learn from the scriptures that God is angry with men until they are restored to his favour by the death of Christ. God freely gives us mercy even though he was our enemy because of our sin.

The Bible clearly tells us that we had brought God's anger upon ourselves which would result in our eternal death. We would be shut off from all hope of salvation, slaves of Satan, captives of sin and doomed to terrible destruction. But with great mercy Christ stepped in to plead for us; took the penalty we deserved; atoned with his own blood for the evil which had made man hateful in God's sight; and laid the foundation for peace between God and man. When we realise the destruction from which he has saved us, we will be more conscious of his mercy than if we had simply been told: "God loved us and would not leave us to be separated from him".

When we were most deeply in sin, the Lord was not willing that any of his own should perish, and graciously loved us. We are his creation, and it is still true that he made us for life. When there was not one attractive thing in us, he — simply because of his own grace and love — took

86

us into his favour again. But our wickedness was not to be reconciled with his righteousness. The two could not live together. God, by the atonement that Christ made on the cross, deals with all the evil in us and treats us as righteous and holy, thus removing all the reasons for our separation from him.

Because he first loved us, God reconciled us to himself through the work of Christ. "In a marvellous and divine manner God loved us, even when he hated us; he saw in us our own handiwork to hate, and his own handiwork to love" (Augustine).

Obedience. Christ reconciled us to God by his whole life and death of obedience. "For as by one man's disobedience many were made sinners, so by one man's obedience many will be made righteous" (Romans 5:19). In fact, Christ began to pay the price for us from the time he became a servant. But the price was even more definitely paid in his death. "the Son of man came . . . to give his life as a ransom for many" (Matthew 20:28). "Christ died for our sins" (I Corinthians 15:3). "Behold the Lamb of God, who takes away the sin of the world" (John 1:29). The obedience in both life and in death can be seen to be necessary as we learn in Philippians 2:7,8 that he "emptied himself, taking the form of a servant, being born in the likeness of men. And being found in human form he humbled himself and became obedient unto death, even death on a cross".

Christ was not an unwilling victim; a sacrifice not freely offered could never justify us. He said about his life: "No man takes it from me, but I lay it down of my own accord" (John 10:18). If Christ had not taken the judgment on himself and accomplished the sentence, we should pass our lives in dread of the judgment of God.

Becoming accursed. It is significant that Christ's death

was by crucifixion. The cross was accursed in man's view and also in God's (see Deuteronomy 21:23). By being placed on the cross, Christ became accursed. The curse due to fall on us for our sins had to fall on him: "The Lord has laid on him the iniquity of us all" (Isaiah 53:6). The cross was the sign of the transfer of sin from us to him. "Christ redeemed us from the curse of the law, having become a curse for us, for it is written, Cursed be everyone who hangs on a tree" (Galatians 3:13,14). By faith we learn that the curse laid on him has resulted in blessing for us.

Death. When Christ died, he took our place. We were in the power of death because of sin. Christ placed himself under the power of death so that he could deliver us from it. He, "by the grace of God, tasted death for everyone" (Hebrews 2:9). It is equally true to say, then, that he died so we would never die, and that he bought our life by his death. Christ took part in death, "that through death he might destroy him who has the power of death, that is, the devil; and deliver all those who through fear of death, were subject to lifelong bondage" (Hebrews 2:14,15).

Burial. There is significance in the fact that Christ was buried. The symbol is that we can be buried from the old life of sin. We are, in a sense, buried with Christ and leave our sinful life behind us.

Descent. In the Apostles' Creed, which many of us say, it states that Christ descended into hell, so let us think of this descent. He had stooped such a very long way from his heavenly glory to the state of being cursed for mankind. And he had to go even lower to do battle with the powers of hell, and fight and conquer eternal death. So now we do not have to dread their terrors, when we die, for Christ has conquered them for us.

Resurrection. The work of Christ in reconciliation, obedience, death, burial and descent would have been useless if he had not risen. Because Christ rose, we too have a living hope. His renewed life shows he is the conqueror of death and as a result of this knowledge we, by faith, may confidently expect victory over death for ourselves. In fact, Christ could not have conquered death for us, if he had been conquered by it.

The fact that our newness of life depends on his resurrection is shown by Paul: "As Christ was raised from the dead by the glory of the Father, we too might walk in newness of life. For if we have been united with him in a death like his, we shall certainly be united with him in a resurrection like his" (Romans 6:4,5). "If you have been raised with Christ, seek the things that are above, where Christ is seated at the right hand of God. Set your minds on things that are above, not on things that are on earth. For you have died, and your life is hid with Christ in God" (Colossians 3:1-3). Christ's resurrection is the firmest promise that we shall also rise. "Christ has been raised from the dead, the first fruits of those who have fallen asleep" (I Corinthians 15:20).

Ascension. Christ's glory began to be shown by his resurrection, but he did not really enter his kingdom of glory until he ascended to heaven. He "ascended far above all the heavens that he might fill all things" (Ephesians 4:10). Here we learn the beautiful harmony of two statements which appear to contradict each other. Christ had said: "You do not always have me" (John 12:8). By this he meant that his body is not with mankind always. But he had also said: "Lo, I am with you always, even unto the end of the world" (Matthew 28:20). The wonderful truth of this is that we have the presence and power of his Spirit.

Coronation. Christ sits at the right hand of God as a sign that he has received all power to rule in heaven and earth. His coronation in heaven has opened the path to God for sinners. Because Christ entered heaven in our nature, we, with him, are able to meet with God. Christ is our advocate, so that with him interceding for us, we are able to approach the throne of God without being filled with terror. And Christ's power as king is fully sufficient to give us the needed strength against the powers of darkness.

Return. At present Christ does rule over the earth, but this reign is to some extent hidden. In the last day he will descend from heaven in visible form, and all men will be able to see his infinite might, the majesty of his kingdom, the splendour of his immortality and the power of his Godhead. We are told to expect that day when he will divide mankind, separating those whom he has chosen from those who are refused.

Judgment. The fact that Christ will judge is a source of fear to those who do not belong to him, but those of us who believe are comforted to know that all judgment is committed to him. He will most certainly not condemn those whom he has appointed to share the judgment with him. Christ, as a merciful sovereign, will most certainly not condemn his own subjects. Christ, as the head of the church, will not scatter the body of the church. Most certainly our advocate will not condemn us, his own clients.

In concluding this section, we affirm that every part of our salvation is completely carried out by Christ. From him and him alone come all the parts of salvation, gifts of the Spirit, strength, consolation, redemption, acquittal, deliverance, newness of life, heavenly inheritance, confidence in his judgment, and abundant supply of every blessing.

Section 17.   Christ merited grace for us.

Some people have said that to use the word "merit" hides the brightness of God's grace to us. But when we speak of merit, we should see both God's grace to us and the work of Christ (his merit) which brought us that grace. The grace of God sent Christ to perform the meritorious work which could bring us salvation. There is no contradiction between the free grace of God and the obedience of Christ. This truth is very clear in the scriptures: "In this is love, not that we loved God, but that he loved us and sent his Son to be the propitiation for our sins" (I John 4:10). God provided the method of reconciliation by Christ so that nothing would stand in the way of his love. Propitiation is the right word since it shows that, in an unexplained way, God was angry with us even while he loved us.

When we state that grace was obtained for us by the merits of Christ, we mean that we are purified by his blood and that his death was the expiation for our sins. "His blood cleanses us from all sin" (I John 1:7). "This is my blood of the covenant, which is poured out for many for the forgiveness of sins" (Matthew 26:28). Our sins are taken from us because, at the cost of his life, Christ satisfied the justice of God. John the Baptist proclaimed this clearly: "Behold, the Lamb of God, which takes away the sin of the world" (John 1:29).

The same truth is taught by the ceremonies of the Jewish law. Without the shedding of blood there was no remission for sin (see Hebrews 9:22). The writer of the letter to the Hebrews develops this when he says: "If the sprinkling of defiled persons with the blood of goats and bulls and with the ashes of an heifer sanctifies for the purification of the flesh, how much more shall the blood of Christ ... purify your conscience from dead works" (Hebrews 9:13,14). This was stated even in Isaiah's time: "The chastisement of our peace was upon him and with his stripes we are healed" (Isaiah 53:5).

We read of both grace and propitiation in two consecutive verses: "Being justified freely by his grace through the redemption that is in Christ Jesus: whom God hath set forth to be a propitiation through faith in his blood" (Romans 3:24,25). The Father's anger is appeased because of his Son: "Your sins are forgiven you for his name's sake" (I John 2:2).

PART III:

THE METHODS AND RESULTS OF RECEIVING THE GRACE OF CHRIST.

Section 1. The gospel of Christ profits us as a result of the secret operation of the Spirit.

Christ's redeeming work will be of no benefit to us if we are not united to him. We can receive the blessings of God, obtained for us by the work of Christ, only through the Spirit. "You were washed, you were sanctified, you were justified in the name of the Lord Jesus Christ and in the Spirit of our God" (I Corinthians 6:11). The Holy Spirit is the bond which ties us to Christ.

Many titles have been given in scripture to the Holy Spirit:

1. He is called the "Spirit of sanctification" because the work of the Holy Spirit causes the beginning of heavenly life in us. This is why the prophets foretold that there would be a much greater pouring out of the Holy Spirit in the kingdom of Christ.

2. He is called both the Spirit of the Father and the Spirit of the Son. Both of these titles are given in the same verse. "But you are not in the flesh, you are in the Spirit, if the Spirit of God really dwells in you. Any one who does not have the Spirit of Christ does not belong to him" (Romans 8:9).

3. The Spirit of adoption. He demonstrates God's free

favour in calling us to be his sons. The Spirit teaches us to have confidence in prayer and to look on God as our Father.

4. The pledge of our inheritance. From heaven and in us he stirs our inner being and assures us that our salvation is certain.

5. The water of life. "I will pour water on the thirsty land, and streams on the dry ground; I will pour my Spirit upon your descendants and my blessing upon your offspring" (Isaiah 44:3).

6. Oil. "You have been anointed by the holy one". "And you have no need that any one should teach you; as his anointing teaches you about everything" (I John 2:20,27). The Spirit sets us apart as those who are taught by God.

7. Fire. The Holy Spirit burns up our impurities and kindles in our hearts the love of God and of godliness. "He will baptise you with the Holy Spirit and with fire" (Luke 3:16).

The special work of the Holy Spirit is to give faith which will bring us into the light of the gospel. John teaches us: "To all who received him, who believed in his name, he gave power to become children of God; who were born, not of blood, nor of the will of the flesh, nor of the will of man, but of God" (John 1:12,13). This contrast of God with flesh and blood points out that the power to receive Christ is a supernatural gift given to those who would otherwise remain unbelievers. The same fact is learnt from the Lord's words to his disciples: "And I will pray the Father and he will give you another counsellor, to be with you for ever, even the Spirit of truth, whom the world cannot receive, because it neither sees him nor knows him; you know him, for he dwells with you and will be in you" (John 14:16,17).

Section 2. Faith and its properties.

We have already shown three important points:
1. The terrible sentence of eternal death hangs over us because we have broken the law which God gave us.
2. It is more than difficult, it is impossible for fallen man to fulfil the law. If we rely on ourselves we have no hope of escaping eternal death.
3. There is only one way to be delivered from this awful calamity. This way is the redemption that is in Christ Jesus. Our heavenly Father promised this redemption to us who rely on his mercy with true faith and firm hope.

We must now look into the meaning of this word "faith". For many people, faith means only the belief in the historical truth of the life of Christ. Even to say that God is the object of faith does not bring us nearer in understanding, because God dwells in light that no man can approach and Christ alone must show us the way to him. Christ calls himself the light of the world, the way and the truth and the life; because no man comes to the Father but by him (John 14:6), and because no man knows the Father but the Son and those to whom the Son wills to reveal him (Luke 10:22).

Paul testifies that the glory of God is to be seen in the person of God's Son, and that the light of the knowledge of the glory of God shines in the face of Jesus Christ (II Corinthians 4:6). Our faith must be in the only true God. Our faith must also rest in Jesus Christ whom he has sent. If the brightness of Christ did not shine on us, God would still be completely hidden from us.

There is no such thing as implicit faith, if by this we simply mean ignorance. Merely to do what the church tells a person to do and to have no understanding is not faith. Faith is not ignorance, but knowledge of God and of his will. Faith consists of knowing God and Christ, not of revering the church. The scriptures everywhere teach that true faith is accompanied by enlightened understanding.

We must also recognise that it is only possible to know Christ, the object of our faith, through the gospel. Our faith must be dependant on the Word of God. The scriptures are "written that you may believe that Jesus is the Christ, the Son of God, and that believing you may have life in his name" (John 20:31). In fact, faith that is not based on the Bible is more likely to be fairy tales and error.

We may wonder what it is in the Word of God that faith should rest on. Faith is not merely a knowledge of God's will; faith consists in knowing his goodwill and mercy. We need his promise of grace to show us that he is our merciful Father. Here then is a correct definition of faith: Faith is a firm and certain knowledge of God's goodwill towards us, a knowledge which is founded on the truth of his gracious promise in Christ revealed to our understanding and sealed upon our heart by the Holy Spirit.

Different uses of the word "faith". We do not want to be confused by the different ways in which this word is used, so we will pick out and differentiate between the various meanings.

1. Some people have stated that there is such a thing as indefinite faith. They use this term of the faith of people who may believe the scripture is true but have no true reverence of God. But Paul has written: "for man believes with his heart and so is justified" (Romans 10:10). If a faith reaches to the head only and not to the heart, it is not true faith at all. Besides, faith is knowledge of Christ who cannot be known without the sanctifying power of His Spirit is the heart and life.

2. Many people believe there is a God and that the history told in scripture is true. These people may even try to obey

the commandments in the Bible, but if there is no genuine obedience to the will of God, their faith is not true faith. They may think they have faith. They think it is real religion to respect the Word of God, but they do not have a living, fruitful and lasting faith.

3. The word "faith" is also used to mean sound doctrine. An example of this occurs when Paul tells Timothy that a good minister of Jesus Christ must be "nourished on the words of the faith and of the good doctrine which you have followed" (I Timothy 4:6).

The nature of true faith.   When we define faith as "firm and certain knowledge" we do not mean the kind of knowledge that we have of things by using our natural senses, but a superior knowledge above the mind of man. Paul writes of "knowing the love of Christ which surpasses knowledge" (Ephesians 3:19). John rightly speaks of faith as knowledge when he testifies that believers know that they are the sons of God (I John 3:2). The knowledge that leads to faith consists of certainty rather than understanding.

Faith seeks full certainty, even though unbelief is so firmly rooted in our hearts that no man becomes fully persuaded of the faithfulness of God without a severe conflict. To remedy this disease of unbelief, the Holy Spirit speaks in high terms of the authority of God's Word: "The promise of the Lord proves true; he is a shield for all those who take refuge in him" (Psalm 18:30).

There are many people who are uncertain whether God will be merciful to them. They see his mercy as great and full, but doubt whether they themselves will ever reach it, and so they are continually troubled by uncertainty. But we do have assurance from the scriptures. Paul says: "In Christ we have boldness and confidence of access through our faith in him" (Ephesians 3:12). A believer possesses a firm conviction that he is reconciled to God and that God is his kind and merciful Father. A true believer confidently says with Paul: "For I am sure that neither death nor life, nor angels, nor principalities nor powers, nor things present, nor things to come, nor height, nor depth, nor anything else in all creation, will be able to separate us from the love of God in Christ Jesus our Lord" (Romans 8:38–39).

Many people experience a wavering in their assurance of God's mercy, and this is to be expected. We are conscious of continuous conflict with our own reluctance to believe, but the true believer never gives up his fixed confidence in the mercy of God. David is a vivid example of this. He was a man with his faith fixed on God, and yet on many occasions he has a strong conflict with unbelief. "Why are you cast down, O my soul, and why are you disquieted within me? Hope in God; for I shall again praise him" (Psalm 42:11; 43:5). "I said in my alarm, 'I am driven far from thy sight'" (Psalm 31:22). It is wonderful that the faith of a godly person in such trials and questionings does rise victorious over the conflict. "Wait for the Lord: be of good courage, and he shall strengthen thine heart" (Psalm 27:14).

We may see the reason for these inner conflicts when we remember that we have already learnt that within the Christian are both flesh and spirit. Christians are happy to know God's goodness and the promise of salvation, but miserable to know their own sinfulness. The Christian's faith while on earth is not yet perfect. That must wait until heaven. But they can rest assured that, even though their faith may be shaken, they will never lose it altogether. "This is the victory that overcomes the world, our faith" (I John 5:4).

There is another kind of fear which is actually good for our faith. When believers tremble as they think of the examples of God punishing evil, they learn to take care in case they cause God's anger by their own wrong-doing. "Therefore, let any one who thinks that he stands take heed lest he fall" (I Corinthains 10:12). In this statement, Paul is warning against overconfidence which trusts in our own strength. There can be no confidence in ourselves when we are told to "work out your own salvation with fear and trembling" (Philippians 2:12).

Our faith relies on the goodwill of God for salvation and eternal life. The nature of God's love means our salvation is absolutely secure. If a rich man is not sure whether God loves or hates him, he will still be miserable. In contrast, even a poor man who is sure of God's love for him will be certain that God will never fail him.

Our definition of faith said that faith is knowledge founded on God's gracious promise, for it is true that faith will grow from his unconditional promises rather than from his commands or threats. God's promises are found in the Bible, but a man will not be able to accept them until he is enlightened by the power of the Holy Spirit, and even after that the Spirit must strengthen his heart and will. God's word is not received by faith while it is understood only with the mind. It must be received into the whole person — heart, emotions and will, so that it will be unconquerable when attacked by the evil one.

This living faith must necessarily be accompanied by the hope of eternal salvation. If we have faith, we believe that God is true and he will be faithful to his promise. He will treat us as his children. If we do not have this certain hope of salvation, neither do we have faith.

But this faith is enough by itself. There is no dual foundation of faith and good works. We rely solely on God's mercy.

Section 3.   True repentance.

There are two main teachings in the gospel: repentance and remission of sins. Both are given by Christ and obtained through faith. We will consider repentance first.

Repentance follows faith and is also a result of faith. A man cannot repent until he has accepted the grace of the gospel. He can only do this if he has faith. When he has accepted the gospel, he will necessarily leave his sinful ways — i.e. he will repent. Repentance and faith are very closely connected but they are not the same thing. Paul writes of them separately: "Repentance toward God and faith toward our Lord Jesus Christ".

The Hebrew word for repentance means turning around or converting, while the Greek word means a change of mind and plan. Both meanings should be included in our definition: Repentance is a true conversion of our life to God, as a result of sincere fear of God. It includes both the putting to death of the flesh and the renewal of the spirit of the mind. There are three points to be considered in this definition.

1.   Conversion to God must mean more than a change in external actions. The heart itself must be changed. This is why Ezekiel, when encouraging the people to repent, spoke of repentance as a matter of the heart: "Cast away from you all the transgressions which you have committed against me, and get yourselves a new heart and a new spirit" (Ezekiel 18:31). Repentance is not true repentance unless the wickedness is removed from the heart.

2.   Repentance is a result of a sincere fear of God. A sinner will not even think about the need to repent until he knows that God is going to judge him. But when he knows that God will judge him, his conscience will make him worried and urge him to turn around in his way of life, and thus repent. True conversion begins with a fear and hatred of

sin. "You were grieved into repenting ... for godly grief produces a repentance that leads to salvation" (II Corinthians 7:9,10).

3. The first part of repentance is the putting to death of the flesh. This is clearly seen in such verses as: "Depart from evil and do good; seek peace, and pursue it" (Psalm 34:14). "Wash yourselves; make yourselves clean; remove the evil of your doings from before my eyes; cease to do evil, learn to do good; seek justice" (Isaiah 1:16,17). It is necessary to do this because "to set the mind on the flesh is death, but to set the mind on the Spirit is life and peace" (Romans 8:6).

The second part of repentance, renewal of the spirit of the mind, is shown in the fruit that springs from the life of the converted person (see Galatians 5:22,23; Philippians 4:8). These things all come to us by union with Christ. If we truly share in his death, our old nature is crucified and we take part in his resurrection, and so we are woken up to a new life. Such repentance is not the matter of a moment or a day or a year. It lasts a life-time. New birth means that a Christian is no longer controlled by sin, though he will still have to fight with his sinful nature. The Christian does not lose his old nature, and this is what makes him still want evil things. He cannot be completely freed from these evil desires until he dies. When God removes sin, he takes away the guilt and penalty of sin. He does not take away the presence of sin. But he does something which will bring us to greater victory — he supplies to Christians the power of the Spirit to conquer sin. We should always remember our own weakness and the need to rely on the Holy Spirit. In Romans 7 Paul is speaking of his experience after he became a Christian and shows us clearly that sin remains in us after we are converted. Paul still felt a dislike for the law of God (verse 23). He knows that nothing good lives in his flesh (verse 18) and that there is the wretchedness of continual conflict because of the sin within him (verse 24).

Some people have taught that the children of God are reborn in salvation to a state of innocence and thus, however much they sin, they will be innocent in God's sight. Because, they say, it is the Holy Spirit who lives now in them, so there is no longer any need for them to curb their lusts. Whatever they do now cannot be sin, being done by the Spirit!— What kind of a Spirit is this? But we can be sure that the Holy Spirit does not encourage murder, immorality, pride, greed or deceit. The Holy Spirit is the source of love, virtue, modesty, peace and truth. The Holy Spirit is given to lead us into the righteousness of God.

In II Corinthians 7:11, Paul speaks of seven signs that show that a man has repented: earnestness, so that he watches to guard against temptation to sin; eagerness to clear himself, an endeavour to give practical proof of his sincerity and reverence for God; indignation, which is anger against himself when he sees his own sinfulness and ungratefulness to God; alarm is the fear he feels when he thinks about the punishment he deserved from such a righteous God; longing, which is probably his great longing to obey God; zeal is also the effect of knowing his own tendency to sin which makes him the more keen to obey God; punishment is the inward shame he feels when he thinks of God's divine judgment on his sin and the punishment he should have received. In summary, we can say that the results of repentance in a life are obedience to God; love to man; and a life which is holy and pure.

The gospel is made up of these two things: repentance and remission of sins. John the Baptist's cry was: "Repent, for the kingdom of heaven is at hand" (Matthew 3:2); and the teaching of Christ was similar: "Repent and believe the gospel" (Mark 1:15).

The Bible teaches that repentance is the gift of God and

not something we can produce in ourselves. In Acts 11:18 repentance is spoken of as something that God had given: "Then to the Gentiles also God has granted repentance unto life". The same is seen in II Timothy 2:25: "God may perhaps grant that they will repent and come to know the truth". God exhorts all men to repent, but these exhortations are effective only where the Holy Spirit brings a man to new life by the new birth.

Repentance is not, strictly speaking, the cause of salvation, but the two are so closely linked as to be inseparable. The Bible does tell us of some who were greatly enlightened and who saw so much of the light of God's truth that they could not plead ignorance. When such people deliberately hardened their hearts and contemptuously rejected God's grace, they were in effect despising the blood of Christ and crucifying the Son of God afresh (Hebrews 6:6). Such apostates could not repent and therefore could not be saved. This sin is called the unforgiveable sin or the sin against the Holy Ghost.

Section 4. An examination of the Roman Catholic doctrine of repentance.

Roman Catholics say that repentance is weeping for past sins and not doing them again; punishing oneself by sorrowing over sin. They think that repentance is severe discipline in order to restrain one's flesh, and a form of punishment. They say nothing about the inward renewing of the person and true reformation of life.

This matter of remission of sins is very important. We must see what the Roman Catholic teaching is and understand what is wrong with it. They say that repentance is made up of sorrow for sin felt with the heart; confession of sin by the mouth; and satisfaction of God's justice by good works. They say that in order to receive forgiveness of sins we must fulfil these three conditions.

1.   Sorrow for sin. Roman Catholic teaching says that sorrow is necessary and that the sorrow must be sufficient and perfect. But how could a man ever know if his sorrow has been sufficient to pay the debt he owes to God? We agree that a man should be sorrowful for his sins, but we do not say that he can be forgiven just because he has sorrowed. Sorrow for sin is not the cause of forgiveness. A sinner's hope is not in his tears but in the mercy of God.

2.   Confession with the mouth. Roman Catholics teach that a sinner must confess his sins to a priest, who will then be able to remove them. They use some passages of scripture wrongly to support their theory. They say that when Christ sent lepers to the priest, leprosy is a picture of sin which must be taken to the priest. Of course, Christ really sent them in obedience to the law which stated that if a leper was cured he had to have the priest's recognition of the fact. Another wrong use of scripture occurs concerning the verse: "Confess your sins one to another, and pray for one another" (James 5:16). This cannot mean that one special man should be confessed to. It obviously speaks of mutual confession and mutual prayer. The relationship of penitent and priest is not found in that verse. The argument that confession is ordered by the law of God has no basis in reality. Confession to a priest is not found in the scriptures, and it was not even fixed in Roman Catholic law until the beginning of the thirteenth century after Christ.

The Bible teaches that only the Lord God can remove sins. He can forget them and blot them out. We have wronged him, so to him we must go to find peace. He calls sinners to his mercy-seat, so we should go to him for mercy. "I acknowledged my sin to thee, and I did not hide my iniquity; I said, 'I will confess my transgressions to the Lord'; then thou didst forgive the guilt of my sin" (Psalm

32:5). "If we confess our sins, he is faithful and just and will forgive our sins, and cleanse us from all unrighteousness". (I John 1:9).

3. Satisfaction of God's justice by works. This is the teaching that the repentant man can make God merciful to him by tears, fasting, giving money, and by charity to others. By doing these things, a man is supposed to pay the debt he owes to God's justice; make up for his own sins; and earn his own pardon. Such teachers say that, although God removes his guilt, God must punish man for the sake of discipline; but man can avoid this by 'satisfaction'. If this is true, then our salvation would not depend on God's mercy alone, but also on our own good works. On the contrary, scripture teaches that forgiveness is free. "He saved us, not because of deeds done by us in righteousness, but in virtue of his own mercy, by the washing of regeneration and renewal in the Holy Spirit" (Titus 3:5). The word "remit" indicates a pure gift. If we say a creditor has remitted a debt we mean he has cancelled it and there is nothing more to pay. In the same way the Lord says: "I am he who blots out your transgressions for my own sake, and I will not remember your sins" (Isaiah 43:25).

Roman Catholics have said that sins can be blotted out when a man is baptised, but that later sin must be made up for by works of satisfaction. But John tells us definitely: "If any man sin, we have an advocate with the Father, Jesus Christ, the righteous" (I John 2:1). Christ is our continual advocate whose intercession always restores us to the Father's favour. John the Baptist said: "Behold the Lamb of God who takes away the sin of the world" (John 1:29). Jesus alone is the Lamb of God and that means he is the only offering for sin.

There is another teaching about sins which we must refute — the fiction that some sins are venial (will not bring death) and some are mortal (will bring death). People who teach this say that we can make up for venial sins by saying the Lord's prayer, being sprinkled with holy water, etc. But this is contrary to scripture for there we are taught that, without any distinctions: "The wages of sin is death" (Romans 6:23). When a believer sins, it will not cause his spiritual death (although that is what he deserves), but this is because God is merciful and does not condemn those who are in Christ Jesus.

One argument that is used to support the teaching of 'satisfaction' for sins is found in the fact that even after David had been forgiven for his sin against Uriah and Bathsheba, God punished him with the death of his son. But God administers two kinds of punishment: correction, and righteous vengeance. The death of David's son was God's corrective, not the pouring out of his curse.

Section 5. Some more Roman Catholic teachings.

The teaching about indulgences is one which we completely reject. This teaching says that there are merits of Christ and the apostles and martyrs stored up as the treasure of the church, and that the Pope and bishops can dispense these to other men. If this were a true doctrine, then sins could be remitted by the merits of apostles and martyrs, but the Bible says: "The blood of Jesus Christ cleanses us from all sin" (I John 1:7). And we are told in Hebrews 10:14: "For by a single offering he has perfected for all time those who are sanctified". Remission of sins could not possibly depend on the blood of martyrs.

Purgatory is the teaching that after a person's death he must make further 'satisfaction' for his sins before he can be received by God. We have already shown that the blood of Jesus is the only means of removal of sins, and that there is no need for further works to 'satisfy' God's justice before

106

a sinner can be saved. So, if there is no place of purgatory, then there is no call to pray for people who have died, for they are already either accepted or rejected by God. The Bible nowhere tells us that we should pray for dead people.

Section 6.   Christian living.

This is a very large subject and I must restrict myself in this book to pointing out the way a godly man should live. The scriptures aim to teach us to love righteousness, and to learn the rules to guide us in our lives and so be kept from error.

We are instructed: "Be ye holy, for your God is holy" (Leviticus 19:1; I Peter 1:16). Holiness must be the bond which binds us in fellowship with God. It is not possible for us to deserve fellowship with God by our holiness, but we must be holy when he is so holy. He can have no fellowship with uncleanness.

To encourage us to holiness, the scriptures tell us that Christ is given as our example. In fact, we stand guilty of the deepest ingratitude if we wish to call God our Father and are not willing to act in a way that is fitting as his sons.

There are some very strong reasons why we should live holy lives for the Lord. Christ has given his blood for us to be washed clean. How wrong it would be to dirty ourselves in more filth. The Holy Spirit has made us temples of God, and we must keep his temples clean. Our soul and body are to receive immortality, so we must take care to preserve them blameless for that day.

A man who calls himself a Christian and makes no effort to live the sanctified life has no right to the name. Paul says that such people must "put off the old nature . . . and put on the new nature, created after the likeness of God in true righteousness and holiness" (Ephesians 4:22–24). I do not

107

mean to say that a Christian is perfect; for nobody could then rightly belong to the church, for none can reach that standard. But such a standard of holiness must be our goal in life.

Section 7.   Christian self-denial.

God has told us that we should "present our bodies a living sacrifice, holy and acceptable to himself", and that this is our "reasonable service" (Romans 12:1). We no longer belong to ourselves, and no longer should our own will or reason take control of our deeds. We are the Lord's; therefore, let his wisdom and will preside over all our actions. Let us put aside our own reason and accept his control, for we will be ruined if we try to work merely by the light of our own reason. If our reason is submitted to the Holy Spirit, then we no longer live for ourselves but Christ lives in us (Galatians 2:20). This submission of our reason makes up the self-denial that Christ asks of his disciples. With that as the guiding principle in a man's life, all greed and self-indulgence will be forced out.

Paul sums up this teaching in writing to Titus; "for the grace of God has appeared for the salvation of all men, training us to renounce irreligion and worldly passions, and to live sober, upright, and godly lives in this world, awaiting our blessed hope, the appearing of the glory of our great God and Saviour Jesus Christ" (Titus 2:11–13). The purpose of salvation is seen in the next verse: "to purify for himself a people of his own who are zealous for good deeds" (Titus 2:14). Paul first encourages our love by telling us of God's grace. Then he removes two obstacles — ungodliness and worldly passions — that would hinder service to God. Then Paul describes the Christian life with three adjectives — sober, upright and godly. Sobriety includes chastity, self-restraint, and honest and careful use of all that God has given us. Righteousness means fairness and honesty in all dealings with other people. Godliness is what makes us different from worldly people and joins us to God in holiness.

Those who long for God's blessing rather than worldy prosperity, will not rely on their own cleverness. They will not be greedy for wealth and honour, but will ask God to give them just what he wants for them in life. This is true self-denial.

Section 8.   Bearing the cross.

In Matthew 16:24, the Lord tells us to take up the cross. By this he means that there is a burden to bear, hardship, hard work, and tribulation. God's Son had to bear such difficulties and Christians must also be proved and exercised by them. "Suffering produces endurance, and endurance produces character and character produces hope" (Romans 5:3,4). God has promised to be with us in suffering and those who suffer like that prove his presence. In this way the cross that we must bear teaches us not to rely on ourselves but on God.

The need to trust in God is the main lesson from suffering, but there are others too. The Lord sometimes sends great difficulties to test out the graces has had given. For this reason, Abraham was asked to sacrifice his promised son, Isaac. Such great tests of faith are like being tested in a fire. "So that the genuineness of your faith, more precious than gold which though perishable is tested by fire may redound to the praise of his glory" (I Peter 1:7). If we had abundance of good things in this life we should grow proud and feel we had no need of God. And at times God has to punish us to correct us so that our lives will be improved. We are told this in Hebrews 12:5,6: "My son, do not regard lightly the discipline of the Lord, nor lose courage when you are punished by him. For the Lord disciplines him whom he loves and chastises every son whom he receives". Besides this, the suffering we have to bear may be persecution for righteousness' sake and this is a great honour when we suffer for his sake.

Section 9.   Looking forward to the life to come.

Our natural inclination is to like the world we know, but God does not want us to cling too firmly to it. He constantly shows us how empty it is by giving us troubles and difficulties. We truly profit from this discipline when we learn that we can never have true happiness in this life. Even the good things of this world will not last and we must wait until we get to heaven to find things that are of permanent value.

Yet although we do not count this present life of high value, we must not hate it. Life is a blessing given us by God.

Believers can rightly and readily think about the life to come in heaven. When we leave this world we shall truly be free. While we are on earth, we are "absent from the Lord" (II Corinthians 5:6), but it will be supreme happiness to enjoy his presence for ever. To be sure, it is natural for us to shrink from death, but for the Christian there is light to overcome this fear because the Christian can turn his thinking towards the resurrection life.

Section 10.   The right use of the present life.

Earth is not our final home. We should use the good things

110

here to help us on our journey. Some good men have realised that these good things can be badly used and forbade the enjoyment of them. This is too austere, but the excesses are equally to be avoided.

Scripture does give general rules to guide us. It is right to use God's gifts when they are used for the right purpose, that is, for our good. Here is an example: God gave us more kinds of food than we need so that we should enjoy them.

We will not entertain the thought that God wants us to have only what we need for this would deprive us of the rightful enjoyment of what God has freely given us.

Section 11.   Justification by faith.

There are two main benefits to us from God's love to us in the giving of his Son Jesus Christ. We have already considered how we are sanctified by his Spirit and led into purity of life. We must now deal more with the fact that we are reconciled to God so that, because of Christ's innocence, God is now not a judge but a kindly Father.

Justification before God means that God considers a man as righteous and therefore accepts him. This is the opposite to the treatment given to a sinner so long as he is regarded as a sinner, for sin is so hateful to God that it causes his rightful anger. In human law courts a man can be regarded as righteous if his innocence is proved. But in God's court even a man who is guilty may be regarded as righteous if his sin is covered. A believer is one whose sin is covered by the blood of Christ.

One could say that a man was justified by works if he were so pure and holy that he deserved that God should call him righteous. But we know from observation and from the Bible that no such person has ever lived. A man can be justified by faith if he, by faith, takes hold of the righteousness of Christ as his covering when he stands before God. Justification is the remission of sins and the reckoning to the sinner of Christ's righteousness.

This is not a doctrine of men but is straight from scripture. "They are justified by his grace as a gift, through the redemption which is in Christ Jesus, whom God put forward as a propitiation by his blood, to be received by faith. This was to show God's righteousness, because in his divine forbearance he had passed over former sins; it was to prove at the present time that he himself is righteous and that he justifies him who has faith in Jesus" (Romans 3:24–26). "For our sake he made him to be sin who knew no sin, so that in him we might become the righteousness of God" (II Corinthians 5:21). The scripture does not teach that justification is partly by faith and partly by works. They are opposed to one another. If we rely on our works, we are not acting in faith. If we have faith in God's mercy we will know that our works are useless to bring us salvation. A writer of former times wrote: "Not to sin is the righteousness of God; to receive pardon from God is the righteousnes of man".

Section 12. God's judgment-seat.

We see our need for free justification clearly only when we consider that we are not to be judged in a human law court but at God's judgment-seat. Man's standards do not reach anywhere near the height of God's perfect standards. He is such a holy judge that "the heavens are not clean in his sight", and who will "by no means clear the guilty". "If thou, O Lord, shouldst mark iniquities, Lord, who could stand?" (Psalm 130:3). His righteousness is far above our understanding. If we could only be saved by obeying everything in his law, we should start trembling in fear now, because "Cursed be everyone who does not abide by all things written in the book of the law and do them" (Galatians 3:10).

Who thinks he could earn his salvation? To think you are as good as other men, or even better than they, is not the point. God's standards are pure holiness. Jesus said to those who thought themselves righteous: "You are those who justify yourselves before men, but God knows your hearts; for what is exalted among men is an abomination in the sight of God" (Luke 16:15). The psalmist had true understanding when he wrote: "Enter not into judgment with thy servant; for no man living is righteous before thee" (Psalm 143:2). When we think about our own guilt, we will become so disgusted with ourselves that we will not think any more that we have any chance of gaining merit by good works. We will throw ourselves on God's mercy. "For God resists the proud, but gives grace to the humble".

Section 13. All the praise must be given to God.

If man could claim to earn his own salvation, he would be claiming some of the glory that rightly belongs to God. Jeremiah cried: "Let not the wise man glory in his wisdom, neither let the mighty man glory in his might; let not the rich man glory in his riches: but let him that glorieth glory in this, that he understandeth and knoweth me, that I am the Lord" (Jeremiah 9:23,24). God is robbed of part of the praise due to him if a man boasts in himself.

A man can experience real peace of mind and heart in the presence of God if he receives righteousness as a free gift. "Who can say 'I have made my heart clean; I am pure from my sin'?" (Proverbs 20:9). His own conscience will tell him that he does not deserve peace with God. His only hope is to be united with Christ by faith and so be freely justified.

Section 14.   True justification.

Men can be divided into four classes: those who worship false gods and do not know the true God; those who claim to be Christians but live unclean lives; hypocrites who make a show of Christianity to cover their wickedness; and those who are born anew by the Spirit of God and aim at holiness.

In the first class, we can find both those who are thoroughly evil and also those who try to live a good life but do not know the one true God. It is certainly better to live a good life and God sometimes gives blessings in this world to such people, not as their reward but to show he approves of good living. However, if they do not acknowledge Christ as God they do not have justification. "He who has the Son has life; he who has not the Son of God has not life" (I John 5:12). "And without faith it is impossible to please him" (Hebrews 11:6).

The second and third classes can be considered together. A man who lives an evil life has not been born again by the Spirit of God. Someone not born again cannot have faith and can be neither reconciled with God nor justified. Even so, many of these people think they are able to do deeds that will be accepted by God and will not admit that they have no righteousness.

In the fourth group are those who do not claim to be righteous in themselves, but they are reckoned to be righteous by reconciliation to God and his pardon of their sins. God's Spirit dwells in them and he purifies their lives, sanctifying them and making them obedient; in fact obedience becomes their main desire, with the promotion of God's glory. But even in these people there is imperfection, for "there is not a righteous man on earth who does good and never sins" (Ecclesiastes 7:20). The Lord's people know that they can have no confidence in the good works they manage to carry out. They look on them only as the gifts of God's goodness, and signs that God has called them.

Section 15.   God's glory and our assurance of salvation.

Even the good works done by a man are defiled and cannot count as merit before God. In fact, when we do good works, it is not in our own strength but through God's grace that they are achieved. Anything in us that can be praised is due to God's grace and the glory is rightly his. But we must not think God is displeased when we do good works for he does reward them generously.

The false teaching that says that men may find salvation by good works has been taught for many generations; but we may completely reject it since the scriptures are so clear: "Whatsoever is not of faith is sin" (Romans 14:23). And it is a shameful thing to say of Christ's completed work on the cross that all he did was to earn for us the opportunity to earn our own salvation, when scripture records that only those who believe in him shall be justified. "They that have the Son have life" (I John 5:12). "He who believes has passed from death unto life" (I John 5:24).

If salvation could be by works we should always be worrying that we had not done enough. But believers already share in Christ's life, and sit with him in heavenly places. They have been translated into the kingdom of God and already possess salvation.

Section 16. Some arguments concerning justification by faith.

Some people have said that our teaching abolishes good works and encourages men to continue in sin.

We contend that our teaching has the opposite effect. It encourages good works. We do not preach a faith that has no good works. Faith and good works belong together. By faith we obtain Christ's righteousness, but we cannot do this without at the same time receiving Christ's santification. Christ is he "whom God made our wisdom, our righteousness and sanctification and redemption" (I Corinthians 1:30). Such sanctification must purify our lives and produce good works. We are not justified *without* good works, but we are not justified *by* good works. And there are very strong motives to encourage us to do good works. We would be extremely ungrateful if we did not love him who first loved us, and want to obey and serve him.

And does our teaching encourage men to continue in sin? We teach that the remission of sin is so costly that men could never buy it. Righteousness is free, but is never cheap. Forgiveness cost Christ his own precious blood and his life. Men who know this will know that when they commit sin they are almost guilty of shedding that precious blood again. Such a truth will lead to a horror of sin much greater than if men thought sin could be covered by more good works.

Section 17. The place of the law.

We are accused of acting as if the Old Testament law was given in vain. There are promises such as this: "And because you hearken to these ordinances, and keep and do them, the Lord your God will keep with you the covenant

116

and the steadfast love which he swore to your fathers to keep" (Deuteronomy 7:12). We need to remember that the curse hangs over all who do not keep the whole law; so the whole human race is convicted by this standard. The only escape is to be delivered from the law, and this deliverance is by faith in the mercy of God in Christ.

Some people claim that the apostle James taught that Abraham was justified by works. Paul said Abraham was justified by faith! But when James wrote, there were people in the church who boasted that they had great faith and yet openly showed by their neglect of good works that they had no real faith. James was showing how useless was their confidence. He uses the word faith to mean their view of faith. James does not mean 'If a man have faith without works', but, 'If a man pretend to have faith, yet neglect works'. He shows later how limited their 'faith' is: "You believe that there is one God; the devils believe that; if there is nothing more than that in your faith, it is no wonder that it does not justify you" (James 2:19). James' real teaching is that those who are truly justified by faith prove their righteousness by obedience and good works. Paul would agree!

Section 18.   Rewards.

There are passages in scripture which affirm that God will give to every man according to his works; but such scriptures do not contradict the truth of justification by faith. God saves by his mercy alone, but after that must come sanctification which, of course, includes good works. So believers are told to "labour for the food that endures unto eternal life" (John 6:27), and at the same time God promises to give this to them. This labour is not instead of grace, but a result of the working of grace in a believer. So

117

the use of the word "reward" in scripture does not mean that salvation is the reward of good works, but that there are rewards in heaven for believers, due simply to God pouring out great blessings on his people. God does not give rewards because he owes them to people who try to do good works. He gives rewards to us because he has promised them. It is the order of events that matters.

Section 19.   Christian liberty.

There are three things which make up Christian liberty.
1.   Believers can be sure of their salvation when they give up any attempt to reach a righteousness based on works and obedience to God's law. No man can be righteous according to the standard of the moral law, so a man must either be condemned or freed from that law. But we are taught to look away from the law as a means of righteousness and look at Christ alone. It is not a matter of how we can be righteous, but how we can be *accounted* righteous. But the law still has a part to play in our lives, for it reminds us of our duty and leads us on towards sanctification.
2.   Being thus free from law-keeping as a source of righteousness, believers nevertheless voluntarily obey God's will. Those who are free from the law gladly obey God, for he has freed them. They obey as sons, sure that their kind Father will accept them, and not like servants whose work is set by their masters every day.
3.   There are some things in our lives which are neither commanded nor forbidden in scripture. As to such things, believers need not be tied by scruples and man-made laws. Believers' consciences are put at rest and they can set aside superstitious scruples. They can then have freedom about foods, holy days, special clothes and so on, according to

their own consciences and need not be restricted by man-made laws. Paul said: "I know and am persuaded by the Lord Jesus, that there is nothing unclean of itself: but to him who considers a thing unclean, to him it is unclean" (Romans 14:14). With these words we are given liberty, so far as is allowed by conscience, to use all things. We should abstain from everything that gives offence to men, but with a clear conscience. Paul says: "If someone says to you, 'This has been offered in sacrifice', then out of consideration for the man who informed you, and for conscience' sake — I mean his conscience, not yours — do not eat it" (II Corinthians 10:28,29). We may use all God's gifts without scruple or pricks of conscience provided we use them for what God intended them.

Section 20. Prayer.

Through prayer we have a way into the treasures which are stored up for us with our heavenly Father who has asked us to pray for whatever we hope for. Prayer is both essential and useful.

Some people argue that God knows all our needs and therefore we do not have to pray for them. God certainly does watch over us and sometimes gives us things before we ask for them, but only when we earnestly seek him do we learn to regard him as our only help in trouble.

There are four rules that will help us to pray correctly:
1. Our minds must be humble when we pray to the one true God.
2. We must truly feel the need for the things we ask for.
3. We must have no pride or confidence in ourselves, for all the glory belongs to God.
4. Although we must humble ourselves, we must be encouraged to pray expecting that God will listen and

answer. Christ commanded: "Whatever you ask in prayer, believe that you will receive it, and you will" (Mark 11:24).

No man is worthy to appear in God's presence; but God has given his own Son to be our mediator so that we can come near with a certainty that requests which are asked in his name will be answered, for God does not refuse his Son.

Some people pray to saints who have died. If departed saints do still pray, they could only bring their prayers through the mediator Christ, so it is madness to ask their intercession and ignore the one mediator who is given.

Exposition of the Lord's Prayer.   The first words of the Lord's prayer remind us that we may only come to God through Christ, for God would not be our Father if Christ had not died to make us his brothers and his Father our Father. John says: "To all who received him, who believed in his name, he gave power to become children of God" (John 1:12). When God is said to be "in heaven", we should not think that he is confined within certain limits. Solomon said: "The heaven and the heaven of heavens cannot contain thee".

The first petition is that God's name might be hallowed. It is a disgrace to mankind that this prayer is even needed. Men should give God the honour due to him, and think and speak of him only with the greatest reverence.

The second petition is "Thy kingdom come". This is a far-reaching request. God reigns in men who deny themselves and follow righteousness. So in this petition we ask God to correct our sinful desires and re-form our nature until it obeys him. So the right way to pray is to begin with oneself, asking to be freed from all that disturbs the rule of the kingdom of God within. After this, we can pray for the enlargement of God's kingdom and the overthrow of God's enemies. God's kingdom will fully come when Christ returns and God will be all in all.

The third petition is for God's will to be done on earth as it is in heaven. This petition depends on the previous request and explains a little more how God will be king in the world.

From the first half of this prayer we learn to pray thinking only of the glory of God and not thinking of ourselves. In the second half we commit ourselves to God for everyday affairs.

The prayer for daily bread does not only mean food. It also means all the physical things we need from God day by day. So, we briefly commit ourselves to him for his care; for nourishment, shelter and preservation.

The fifth and sixth petitions ask for what we need to obtain eternal life: forgiveness of sins and victory over temptation. Sins are called 'debts' here because we are bound to pay the penalty for them but, of course, we could not pay and so must be released by forgiveness. "Lead us not into temptation but deliver us from evil" is a prayer for God's strength to be ours, leading to victory over our enemies. Delivery from evil will mean both delivery from the evil one and from sin, for sin is the weapon used against us by our enemy Satan.

This exposition of the Lord's Prayer does not mean that this exact form of words is the only prayer we should say. There are many different prayers in the Bible and many different words inspired by the same Holy Spirit. But we can note that this prayer is an idea of the kind of things we may properly pray for.

Section 21. Election.

God has obviously not chosen everyone for salvation. The gospel is not even preached in every part of the world, and where it is heard not everyone receives it. We have to believe that God elects and predestines certain people. God does not bring everyone without exception into salvation. What he gives to some he denies to others. That contrast sheds light on God's grace by revealing his loving choice of some.

Paul wrote: "There is a rement, chosen by grace. But if it is by grace, it is no longer on the basis of works" (Romans 11:5,6). Paul felt a need to remind us of our election in order to show us that salvation is by grace alone. Those who reject the doctrine of election are also doing away with humility, for it takes real humility to see that we could not even start to turn ourselves to God. The ungodly scorn this doctrine, but that is no reason for us to conceal the truth.

People often have taught that God's election depends merely on his foreknowledge, so that he chooses only those whom he knows beforehand are going to turn to him. But, while believing firmly in God's foreknowledge, we teach that his election goes further than this. Eternal life is fore-ordained for some, eternal condemnation for others, and so all people are predestined for either life or death.

God predestined one race in the same way as he predestined individuals. So here is an example of the way he works. Moses told the people of Israel that the only reason they were chosen was the free love of God. "It was not because you were more in number than any other people that the Lord set his love upon you and chose you, for you were the fewest of all peoples; but it is because the Lord loves you, and is keeping the oath which he swore to your fathers" (Deuteronomy 7:7,8). When we see that God chose one nation just to show his favour on even those who were stubborn and disobedient, we have no right to argue with his judgment when he was pleased to show mercy to individuals.

We must also consider that God not only offers

salvation to individuals, but also makes its reception certain. The members of the family of Christ are an excellent display of God's grace because, once united to him, they can never lose their salvation.

Sections 22,23,24.   More on election.

Many people teach that God knew beforehand that some would be worthy of his grace and chose these as his children. But Paul teaches that "He chose us in him before the foundation of the world that we should be holy blameless before him" (Ephesians 1:4). God was not dealing with us as we deserved. When he chose us so that we should be holy, he did not choose us because he foresaw that we would be holy.

The fact of predestination is clearly taught by the Lord Jesus himself. "All that the Father gives me shall come to me". "This is the will of the Father that of all which he hath given me, I should lose nothing" (John 6:37,39). "No man can come to me, except the Father which has sent me draw him" (John 6:44).

The message of the gospel is proclaimed to all, and some people say God would contradict himself if he invited all men to come to him, but only received a chosen few. But by the preaching of the gospel all men are called to repent. However, the spirit of repentance and belief is not given to all. The gift of faith is rare; but this does not lessen the guilt of unbelief. Paul in Romans 9:20,21 silences those who say that this is unjust. Predestination is very obviously taught in Romans 9 where we are told definitely that before they were born, God said: "Jacob have I loved but Esau have I hated".

Three of the arguments used against predestination need answering here.

1. That God shows favouritism in not dealing with everyone alike. But we say that all men are guilty and God has a right to inflict judgment. He is merciful and saves some.

2. That belief in predestination leads to neglect of good works, since people can claim that it does not matter what they do if God has already decided whether they will be saved or rejected. But the teaching of scripture is totally against such wickedness.

3. That there is no need to preach that we should live good lives, for goodness would make no difference. We have seen that Paul preached election very plainly but he was no less strong in his appeals to live a sanctified life.

Augustine wisely taught people: "Since we know not who the elect are, it is wise for us sincerely to desire the salvation of all, and thus desire to make every person we meet a partaker of peace. But our peace will rest upon the sons of peace".

Section 25. The resurrection.

Christians can know that the only perfect happiness is in union with Christ even while they are on earth. "For our commonwealth is in heaven, and from it we await a Saviour, the Lord Jesus Christ, who will change our lowly body to be like his glorious body" (Philippians 3:20). The matter of the resurrection of the dead is vital, for if the dead do not rise the whole gospel teaching is false (I Corinthians 15:14–19). We may find it difficult to believe that rotted bodies will rise again, but the Bible gives us two helps to encourage our faith.

1. Christ is the assurance we have that we shall rise again, because he took on a human nature, lived his life on earth, and through death reached immortality. "If the dead rise

not, then Christ rose not" (II Corinthians 15:13). Christ rose as the head, the beginning, of what is to be accomplished in all believers.

2. God is omnipotent (all powerful), and so is able to perform what he promises: "He will change our lowly body to be like his glorious body, by the power which enables him even to subject all things to himself" (Philippians 3:21). This is not difficult to believe if we study the wonders of the world around us and if we remember that our glorious God works miracles.

The ungodly will rise again, as well as believers. But to the ungodly will come the terrible vengeance of God which there are hardly words to describe. This vengeance is spoken of as physical torment in the Bible, and this is an indication of how dreadful it will be for them. But the worst punishment will be separation from God. Paul writes very seriously in II Thessalonians 1:9 when he says that unbelievers "shall suffer the punishment of eternal destruction and exclusion from the presence of the Lord and from the glory of his might".

"Who considers the power of thy anger, and thy wrath according to the fear of thee? So teach us to number our days that we may get a heart of wisdom" (Psalm 90:11–12).